Informing Patients

An assessment of the quality of patient information materials

Informing Patients

An assessment of the quality of patient information materials

Angela Coulter
Director of Policy and Development, King's Fund

Vikki Entwistle
Research Fellow, NHS Centre for Reviews and Dissemination, University of York

David Gilbert
Research Officer, King's Fund

Published by
King's Fund Publishing
11–13 Cavendish Square
London W1M 0AN

First published 1998

ISBN 1 85717 214 0

A CIP catalogue record for this book is available from the British Library

Available from:

King's Fund Bookshop
11–13 Cavendish Square
London W1M 0AN

Tel: 0171 307 2591
Fax: 0171 307 2801

Printed and bound in Great Britain

Cover illustration: Minuche Mazumdar Farrar

Contents

Acknowledgements

This study would not have been possible without the enthusiastic co-operation of the focus group participants and the clinical and academic specialists. We thank them for all their help. Caroline Shiffner played a key role in helping to organise the study and we are most grateful for her hard work. The study was funded by the National NHS Research and Development Programme on evaluating methods to promote the implementation of research findings and by the King's Fund.

Note on terminology

Views differ on the most appropriate term to describe people who use health care services. We have chosen to use the term *patients* in this report, in preference to the alternatives *consumers, clients, customers, users,* or *lay people,* mainly because we were reviewing materials intended for use in clinical settings and this is the term most commonly used in that situation.

Executive summary

The *Patient's Charter* promised patients the right to information about their health care and the opportunity to be involved in decisions about their treatment if they so wished.

There is plenty of evidence that patients want information about medical conditions and treatments. Most find it difficult to access the information they need. Most patients would like health professionals to take account of their preferences and many, but not all, want clinicians to involve them in decisions about their care.

Good quality information for patients about health problems can help:

- in preventing disease;
- in promoting self-care;
- in supporting treatment choices;
- in improving the effectiveness of clinical care.

We conducted a study to assess the quality of patient information materials. We organised reviews of selected materials by groups of patients who had experienced specific health problems and by clinical and academic specialists with relevant expertise. Fifty-four materials (leaflets, videos, audiotapes) were reviewed by 62 patients and 28 specialists.

Patients reported needing and using information for a variety of purposes:

- to understand what is wrong;
- to gain a realistic idea of prognosis;
- to make the most of consultations;
- to understand the processes and likely outcomes of possible tests and treatments;
- to assist in self-care;
- to learn about available services and sources of help;
- to provide reassurance and help to cope;
- to help others understand;

- to legitimise help-seeking and concerns;
- to identify further information and self-help groups;
- to identify the 'best' health care providers.

Without good quality information people cannot give informed consent to proposed treatments and are less able to participate in treatment decision-making.

The results of the study give cause for concern about the quality of information currently available:

- Patients want information about treatment options and outcomes even if they do not want to participate in treatment decisions – most don't receive it.
- The quality of most patient information materials is poor.
- Many materials contain inaccurate and out-of-date information.
- Few provide adequate information about treatment risks and side-effects.
- Topics of relevance to patients are omitted.
- Technical terms are not explained.
- Coverage of treatment options is incomplete.
- Uncertainties are ignored or glossed over.
- Information about treatment effectiveness is often missing or unreliable.
- Few materials actively promote shared decision-making.

Access to appropriate information can empower patients to express their treatment preferences and help professionals to improve the information base of clinical decisions. We therefore urge the NHS Executive to take the lead by:

- funding the development and evaluation of high quality patient information materials covering common clinical conditions;
- commissioning patient information materials to accompany the evidence-based clinical guidelines developed by the National Institute of Clinical Excellence;
- establishing a system for accrediting patient information materials and Web sites to assist patients and health professionals seeking reliable information.

Health authorities should support the process by:

- establishing systems for disseminating good quality patient information via GP surgeries, hospital departments, community pharmacies, consumer health information services, healthy living centres and public libraries;

- ensuring that each NHS trust and primary care group has a designated senior member of staff responsible for ensuring that patient information materials meet high quality standards;
- ensuring that all clinicians receive training in communication skills and shared decision-making.

Developers of patient information materials should take account of the following guidelines:

The process

1. Involve patients throughout the process.
2. Involve a wide range of clinical experts.
3. Be specific about the purpose of the information and the target audience.
4. Consider the information needs of minority groups.
5. Review the clinical research evidence and use systematic reviews wherever possible.
6. Plan how the materials can be used within a wider programme promoting shared decision-making.
7. Consider cost and feasibility of distribution and updating when choosing media.
8. Develop a strategy for distribution.
9. Evaluate the materials and their use.
10. Make arrangements for periodic review and updating.
11. Publicise the availability of the information materials.

The content

1. Use patients' questions as the starting point.
2. Ensure that common concerns and misconceptions are addressed.
3. Refer to all relevant treatment or management options.
4. Include honest information about benefits and risks.
5. Include quantitative information where possible.
6. Include checklists and questions to ask the doctor.
7. Include sources of further information.
8. Use non-alarmist, non-patronising language in active rather than passive voice.
9. Design should be structured and concise with good illustrations.
10. Be explicit about authorship and sponsorship.
11. Include reference to sources and strength of evidence.
12. Include the publication date.

Part 1

Assessing the quality of patient information materials

Chapter 1

Uses of patient information

There is increasing enthusiasm for involving patients more closely in decisions about their health care. The *Patient's Charter* informed patients they had a right:

'to be given a clear explanation of any treatment proposed, including any risks and any alternatives, before you decide whether you will agree to the treatment'. (Department of Health 1992)

The *Patient's Charter* for Scotland told patients:

'You are entitled to be involved so far as is practical in making decisions about your own care, and wherever possible given choices'. (National Health Service in Scotland 1991)

The NHS Executive's Patient Partnership strategy was launched in June 1996 in an attempt to make the expressed commitment to user involvement a practical reality (NHS Executive 1996). As well as promoting user involvement in service development and policy-making, the Patient Partnership strategy had the following aims in relation to clinical practice:

- to promote users' involvement in their own care, as active partners with professionals;
- to enable patients to become informed about their treatment and care, and to make informed decisions and choices about it if they wish.

The desire to encourage patient participation stems in part from a belief in the ethical principle of autonomy, but also from the hope that it will promote greater clinical effectiveness and more appropriate and efficient use of resources. These motivations could conflict if patients opted for treatments which professionals did not consider cost-effective, but there are grounds for believing that the effects of greater patient involvement may be beneficial. It has long been known that there is a positive relationship between communication and clinical outcomes (Ley 1988). In 1991 an international

BOX 1 THE TORONTO CONSENSUS STATEMENT ON THE RELATIONSHIP BETWEEN COMMUNICATION PRACTICES AND OUTCOMES

■ Communication problems in medical practice are both important and common.

■ Patient anxiety and dissatisfaction is related to uncertainty and lack of information, explanation and feedback from the doctor.

■ Doctors often misperceive the amount and type of information patients want.

■ The quality of clinical communication is related to positive health outcomes.

■ Explaining and understanding patient concerns, even when they cannot be resolved, results in a significant fall in anxiety.

■ Greater participation by the patient in the encounter improves satisfaction and compliance and outcome of treatment.

■ The level of psychological distress in patients with serious illness is less when they perceive themselves to have received adequate information.

■ Beneficial clinical communication is feasible routinely in clinical practice and can be achieved during normal clinical encounters, without unduly prolonging them, provided that the clinician has learned the relevant techniques.

Source: Simpson *et al.* 1991

conference on doctor-patient communication published a consensus statement which made the points listed in Box 1.

In attempting to reconcile the growing demand for health care with the need to control expenditure, policy makers are beginning to recognise that patient empowerment could have an important part to play. Relationships between professionals and patients in the National Health Service tend to be paternalistic in nature, encouraging dependence on health professionals and fostering demand, sometimes inappropriately. The key role of patients as producers of their own health is often ignored and indeed undermined, leading to inefficient use of resources.

If this problem is to be tackled, it will be necessary to redress the information imbalance between lay people and professionals. Ways will have to be found to provide people with the information they need to be active participants in their care rather than simply passive recipients. Health professionals will have to be trained to take account of patients' views and preferences and to share decision-making in appropriate ways.

Previous research has shown that patients find it difficult to obtain the information they need to participate in decisions about their health care (Audit Commission 1993). There may be various reasons for this. Sometimes health professionals underestimate patients' desire for and ability to cope with information. Consultation times in primary and secondary care are limited and there is often insufficient time to fully explain the condition and treatment choices. Health professionals may themselves lack knowledge of treatment options and their effects. One solution to these problems is to ensure that patients have access to printed or audiovisual material to inform themselves and to use in discussion with health professionals.

Recent years have seen a rapid growth in the availability of patient information materials, including leaflets, videos and multi-media technology, and of course the World Wide Web, which carries a huge amount of health information. From a health policy perspective, health information designed for members of the public can serve a number of purposes: to promote better health and prevent disease, to encourage self-care and reduce inappropriate service use, to ensure the appropriateness of treatment decisions, and to improve the effectiveness of clinical care. Poor information, or misinformation, may adversely affect these areas of health behaviour and health. Some examples of studies demonstrating the uses and effects of information in each of these areas are outlined below.

Information about health promotion and disease prevention

This is the traditional territory of health education, which has been the subject of government investment over many years. In addition to specific campaigns and educational programmes, the Health Education Authority, the Health Education Board for Scotland, and similar bodies hold large stocks of information materials which provide information on disease risks and how to avoid them.

Health education materials have been designed to promote lifestyle change, to modify specific risk factors, and to meet the needs of specific population groups (Health Education Authority 1994, 1995, 1997). Appropriate use of these materials can be effective as part of a primary prevention strategy (Simons-Morton et al. 1992, Kok et al. 1997). For example, information materials have been useful in dental health education (Kay and Locker 1996) and in nutrition education (Contento et al. 1995) and they have a part to play in programmes to reduce heart disease risk (Mullen et al. 1992). Despite the long history of developing health education materials, there is a paucity of good studies of their efficacy in reducing the risk of disease (NHS Centre for Reviews and Dissemination 1995).

Education about the effects of illness, how to recognise symptoms, and when to seek medical help, has a part to play in secondary prevention to ameliorate the impact of disease and prevent recurrence. For example, information materials have been shown to have a useful effect on uptake of screening programmes (Stewart *et al*. 1994) and vaccination programmes (Carter *et al*. 1986) and in control of sexually transmitted diseases (Healton and Messeri 1992).

Information about self-care

The majority of ill health is self-managed (Hannay 1979). Most of us cope with minor illness without recourse to professional help, but the decision about when to consult can be difficult. In the USA the distribution of self-help information has attracted federal and state government funding, but there have not yet been any large-scale publicly-funded attempts to promote self-care in the UK. US examples include the Healthwise patient education programme in Idaho, which aimed to assist people to look after themselves and make appropriate decisions about when to seek professional help (Kemper 1997). Each household in the State was provided with a self-care manual covering common health problems, resulting in reported improvements in appropriate use of services. A similar programme in Rhode Island led to a 35 per cent reduction in primary care consultation rates (Vickery *et al*. 1983). In Oregon the Informed Patient Decisions Group publishes resource guides on patient information materials (Kieschnick *et al*. 1996) and the Agency for Health Care Policy and Research in the US Department of Health and Human Sciences has published a series of consumer guides on specific illnesses.

Telephone advice lines have been extensively used in the USA to promote self-care. It has been estimated that 12–28 per cent of primary care in America is conducted over the telephone (Yanovski *et al*. 1992). Telephone consultations with primary care nurses are also a feature of the Swedish health system (Marklund *et al*. 1991). In Britain the consumer health information services funded by health authorities, have been receiving an increasing number of enquiries about medical treatments, a demand which they are not really resourced to cope with and which their staff have difficulty in meeting (Buckland and Gann 1997). The announcement in the government's White Paper on the NHS (Secretary of State for Health 1997) of the establishment of a national telephone advice service, NHS Direct, was widely welcomed.

This will provide an opportunity to build on the experience of small-scale pilot studies which have pointed to the potential usefulness of these systems in the UK context (Hallam 1993, Williams *et al.* 1995, Brown and Armstrong 1995).

Management of chronic diseases such as asthma, diabetes and epilepsy usually requires active involvement by patients in self-medication and monitoring. Information materials have a part to play in enhancing the ability of patients to manage their treatment (Mullen *et al.* 1985, Brown 1988, Padgett *et al.* 1988, Brown 1990, Gibson *et al.* 1997). For example, a self-help manual has been used as part of a programme to enhance sense of control and self-efficacy in arthritis sufferers, leading to beneficial outcomes (Lorig and Fries 1995). Self-help packages have been used to reduce symptom levels in patients suffering from stress-related psychological problems (Kiely and McPherson 1986) and leaflets have been shown to increase patients' knowledge of hypertension (Watkins *et al.* 1987), and gastrointestinal diseases (Hawkey and Hawkey 1989) and how to take medicines correctly (Gibbs *et al.* 1989).

Video can be an effective educational tool for patients with a variety of conditions, leading to knowledge gain, skills development, or behaviour change (Nielsen and Sheppard 1988, Hopper *et al.* 1994) although the quality of the studies to evaluate the effectiveness of video for health education has generally been poor (Eiser and Eiser 1996). Multi-media packages have been used to educate patients in self-help, for example for urinary incontinence (Niewijk and Weijts 1997) and to prepare patients for radiotherapy treatment (Rainey 1985).

Information about treatment options

If clinicians are ignorant of patients' values and preferences, patients may receive treatment which is inappropriate to their needs. Studies have shown that doctors sometimes fail to understand patients' preferences, leading to inappropriate treatment decisions (Strull *et al.* 1984, Coulter *et al.* 1994, Cockburn and Pit 1997). Shared decision-making, in which patients and health professionals share both the process of decision-making and ownership of the decision made, is attracting considerable interest as a means by which patients' preferences can be incorporated into clinical decision-making (Coulter 1997). The concept of shared decision-making and its place in the spectrum of models of decision-making, is discussed in more detail in the next section (pp. 9–11).

Patients cannot express informed preferences unless they are provided with sufficient and appropriate information. Ideally patients who want it should be given detailed explanations about their condition and the likely outcomes with and without treatment. Information about the risks and benefits of treatment options should be derived from the best and most up-to-date scientific evidence.

Evaluation studies have shown that the provision of information materials can have positive effects on the pattern of care. For example, leaflets providing information about back pain and its treatment have been found to reduce consultation rates and subsequent referrals (Roland and Dixon 1989). Provision of printed information materials has also been found to reduce the rate of hospital admissions for asthma patients (Osman *et al.* 1994), to reduce the rate of reconsultations for acute lower respiratory tract illness (Macfarlane *et al.* 1997) and to improve follow-up of patients with abnormal results in screening programmes (Lerman *et al.* 1992, Stewart *et al.* 1994).

Interactive videos and decision boards have been devised to help patients make treatment choices for a number of conditions, including benign prostatic hyperplasia (Kasper *et al.* 1992, Wagner *et al.* 1995, Barry *et al.* 1995, Barry *et al.* 1997), third molar extraction (Ader *et al.* 1992), breast cancer treatment (Levine *et al.* 1992, Whelan *et al.* 1995) and ischaemic heart disease (Liao *et al.* 1996). Patients given access to videos or scripted information about the pros and cons of prostate cancer screening have been found to be less likely to want to undergo screening tests (Flood *et al.* 1996, Wolf *et al.* 1996).

Information to improve the effectiveness of clinical care

There is some evidence which suggests that giving patients information and encouraging them to participate in treatment decisions can lead to improvements in doctor-patient relationships, health status and quality of life (Brody *et al.* 1989, Lerman *et al.* 1990, Devine 1992, Stewart 1995, Balas *et al.* 1996).

In situations where there are several treatment options with different possible outcomes, particularly those that are likely to have differential effects on the patient's quality of life, there is a strong case for offering patients choice and actively involving them in the decision. This may increase the effectiveness of the treatment. Randomised controlled trials are currently under way to test this hypothesis formally, but a few studies suggest that optimism may be justified. For example, patients with hypertension seem to benefit if they are allowed to adopt an active rather than a passive role in the treatment process

(Schulman 1979, England and Evans 1992) and patients with breast cancer appear to suffer less depression and anxiety if they are treated by physicians who adopt a participative consultation style (Fallowfield *et al.* 1990).

Kaplan and colleagues carried out a series of studies in which patients with different conditions (ulcer disease, hypertension, diabetes and breast cancer) were randomised to an educational intervention in which they were given information about treatment options and coached to ask appropriate questions in the consultation (Kaplan *et al.* 1989). Consultation times did not differ between the two groups, but the group who had received coaching were more involved in the interaction and had significantly better health outcomes measured physiologically (blood pressure and blood sugar), functionally (activities of daily living), or subjectively (evaluation of overall health status).

Although there is a growing body of literature on the subject of patient information and its effects, the majority of the published studies are North American and the methodological quality of many is weak. There is a great need for more and better research to evaluate the effects of using this information in the UK.

Models of clinical decision-making

A hundred years ago doctors expected patients to follow their advice without question. Patients' views and preferences were seen as irrelevant and requests for additional information could be dismissed. In 1871 Oliver Wendell Holmes gave the following advice to US medical students:

> 'Your patient has no more right to all the truth you know than he has to all the medicine in your saddlebags … He should get only just so much as is good for him …' (quoted in Laine and Davidoff 1996)

Relationships between clinicians and patients are very different nowadays. Patients are more likely to challenge the notion that 'doctor knows best' and they expect to be given information about their condition and the treatment options. The doctor-patient relationship seems to be shifting away from the traditional paternalistic model towards a new type of decision-making which gives patients much more say. The traditional model assumed that doctors and patients shared the same goals and that only the doctor was sufficiently informed and experienced to decide what should be done. Patient involvement was limited to giving or withholding consent to treatment.

Professional choice	Professional-as-agent	Shared decision-making	Consumer choice
Clinician decides, patient consents	Clinician elicits patient's views, then makes decision	Information shared, both decide together	Clinician informs, patient makes decision

Fig. 1   Models of clinical decision-making

A number of writers have described different models of decision-making used in present-day clinical settings (Szasz and Hollender 1956, Veatch 1972, Quill 1983, Emanuel and Emanuel 1992, Deber 1994, Charles *et al.* 1997). At least four broad models can be distinguished: professional choice, consumer choice, the professional-as-agent, and shared decision-making (Fig. 1).

The consumer choice model is the polar opposite of the traditional or professional choice model, in that it assumes that the patient alone will make the decision once he/she has been provided with all necessary technical information. Thus the patient's preferences are pre-eminent and the clinician's role is reduced to that of providing technical information and delivering the treatment of the patient's choosing. The professional-as-agent model is somewhere between these two extremes, in that it recognises the importance of incorporating the patient's preferences into the process, but still leaves the clinician to make the final treatment decision. The decision remains with the clinician and is not, therefore, a shared one. In shared decision-making, however, patients and health professionals share both the process of decision-making and ownership of the decision made. Shared information about values and likely treatment outcomes is an essential prerequisite, but the process also depends on a commitment from both parties to engage in a negotiated decision-making process. The clinician has to be prepared to acknowledge the legitimacy of the patient's preferences and the patient has to accept shared responsibility for the treatment decision.

It would be wrong to imply any value judgement about the relative desirability of the different models. All have their place in clinical situations – the trick is to match the appropriate decision-making style to the patient's needs at any particular time. For example, emergency situations often require clinicians to make quick decisions when there is no time to involve the patient. In these cases the professional choice model is entirely appropriate. In other situations it may be appropriate to leave the final decision to the patient, with the clinician's role relegated to provider of technical information as implied in the consumer choice model. Examples might include a woman's choice of contraceptive method – assuming she has full information about efficacy and risks and there are no relevant contra-indications, the woman who wants to should be allowed to decide for herself.

In treating a serious or life-threatening condition, the clinician has to use his or her knowledge of the individual patient to determine the most appropriate style of decision-making. In most cases the choice will be between trying to elicit the patient's preferences and using this information to decide on the most appropriate treatment, or actively involving the patient in the decision. The provision of reliable and clear information is central to both of these approaches.

Do patients want to participate in treatment decisions?

We know patients want more information than they currently tend to be given, but what is the evidence that they want to participate in decisions about their care? Failures in communication of information about illness and treatment are the most frequent source of dissatisfaction, but this does not necessarily mean that patients want to participate in decision-making.

A variety of instruments have been used to elicit patients' role preferences. They vary among other things in the extent to which they imply that people will have access to the information needed to participate in a decision, and also in the extent to which they distinguish between problem-solving (e.g. identifying what the treatment options are) and decision-making (e.g. choosing between the options) (Deber *et al.* 1996). Thus the instruments themselves affect the preferences elicited.

A number of studies have investigated the extent of desire for participation among different groups of patients. For example, in a study of 439 interactions between adult cancer patients and oncologists in a US hospital, the majority (92 per cent) preferred to be given all information including bad news and two-thirds (69 per cent) said they wanted to participate in treatment decisions (Blanchard *et al.* 1988). However, only a minority of patients appear to want the responsibility of making treatment decisions on their own. A Canadian study looked at information and participation preferences among 52 outpatients undergoing post-surgical treatment for cancer (Sutherland *et al.* 1989). Almost two-thirds (63 per cent) felt the doctor should take the primary responsibility in decision-making, 27 per cent felt it should be an equally shared process, and 10 per cent felt they should take the major role.

Desire for participation has been found to vary according to age, educational status, disease group and cultural background. A study of 256 US cancer patients found that younger patients were much more likely to want active participation in decisions about their care: 87 per cent of patients aged under 40 expressed a desire to participate, compared to 62 per cent of those aged 40–59 and 51 per cent of those aged over 60 (Cassileth et al. 1980). The age differences in decision-making preferences suggest that the preference for active involvement may be increasing over time, reflecting greater knowledge of the risks as well as the benefits of medical care and decreased willingness to submit to the authority of clinicians. Alternatively, it may be the case that as people get older they want to take less responsibility for health care decisions. Preference for an active role in decision-making may also vary according to the stage in the course of a disease episode and the severity of the patient's condition. There may also be important cultural differences. Studies comparing responses in different countries found that British breast cancer patients were less likely to prefer an active role than Canadian ones (Richards et al. 1995, Beaver et al. 1996). Although many patients want to participate in decision-making, it is important to remember that a substantial minority prefer a passive role.

Chapter 2

Accessibility of patient information

Despite a national policy commitment to provide patients with information and the opportunity to participate in decision-making, surveys reveal that lack of information is patients' most frequently voiced complaint (Bruster *et al.* 1994, Calnan *et al.* 1994, Sitzia and Wood 1997).

In 1993 the Audit Commission carried out a study of communication between hospitals and patients (Audit Commission 1993). The effectiveness of clinical communication was investigated in this study by looking at the experience of patients with one of four tracer conditions: benign prostatic hyperplasia, breast cancer, rheumatoid arthritis, stroke. This revealed a number of problems (Box 2):

BOX 2   CLINICAL COMMUNICATION: PROBLEMS WITH WRITTEN INFORMATION

Patients:

■ do not get written information about the condition, treatment, procedures and post-operative care;

■ get poor quality information;

■ get information too late to be of use.

Patients and their relatives:

■ do not get information about aids, equipment, and people who can help.

Source: Audit Commission 1993, p.70

The report made a number of recommendations for improving the accessibility and use of written information for hospital patients (Box 3):

Unfortunately there has been no follow-up to this study to ascertain the extent to which hospital staff have complied with the Audit Commission's recommendations.

> ### Box 3 Audit Commission's recommendations for improving written information
>
> Clinical staff and general managers should work together to:
>
> - review the written information currently distributed and the distribution mechanisms;
>
> - find out what kind of information patients and relatives would like;
>
> - provide written information about conditions, procedures and post-operative care;
>
> - make written information from national organisations available;
>
> - allocate resources to the production or purchase of written information;
>
> - make clear arrangements for distributing written information at the right time – for example, before a decision is made about surgery or before discharge from hospital – and check at regular intervals that they work.

The growth and wider availability of the Internet will greatly increase access to health information. It is estimated that the number of users will grow from 33.4 million worldwide in 1996 to 233 million by the year 2000 (Wallace 1996). Currently only 13 per cent of adults in Britain have access to the Internet, but this proportion is likely to grow fast. There are already more than 10,000 health-related Web sites and more than a third of Internet users access the Web to retrieve health and medical information (Rippen 1997). Accessing reliable information on the Internet is not easy and the design of many Web sites and search engines is not particularly user friendly (Agbamu and Sim 1997). Information on the Internet does however have the advantage that it can be updated relatively easily. Combined packages using, for example, links between computer-based packages such as CD-Roms and Web sites, allow for a combination of sound and video, computer graphics and up-to-date information and discussion groups over the Net. Meanwhile, more conventional printed forms of information are becoming increasingly sophisticated and the commercial market for health information appears to be expanding.

The growing demand for patient information increases the need for careful evaluation of the available materials and the development of quality assurance programmes to ensure that people are not misled by inaccurate information.

Chapter 3

Content of patient information

It is clear that patients would welcome the wider availability of information materials, but greater accessibility is of little use if the presentation and content of the materials is poor. There is a long tradition of evaluating the readability and comprehensibility of health education materials using specially devised formulae (Meade and Smith 1991, Meade *et al.* 1992, Arthur 1995, Mumford 1997). Others have focused on aspects of the design of patient information materials to enhance learning outcomes (Vahabi and Ferris 1995, Bernier 1996), or on the way in which information is presented or 'framed' (Malenka *et al.* 1993, Mazur and Merz 1993, North East Thames Regional Health Authority 1994, Secker and Pollard 1995).

Studies of the content of patient information materials are less common. Some examples include an evaluation of leaflets produced by the Arthritis and Rheumatism Council (Bishop *et al.* 1996), a study of 25 factsheets on prostate surgery (Meredith *et al.* 1995), and an evaluation of the reliability of information on the World Wide Web relating to home management of feverish children (Impicciatore *et al.* 1997). These last two studies found many shortcomings in the material presented: topics of relevance to patients were omitted, terminology was often unclear, and much of the information was inaccurate.

A recent study produced and validated a structured instrument (Division of Public Health and Primary Care, University of Oxford 1998) for judging the quality of written information on treatment choices. This consists of a series of questions for use with a simple rating scale. Topics covered include the aims of providing the information, its relevance, reference to sources of evidence, timeliness, balance and bias, sources of further information, reference to uncertainties, description of treatment method, benefits and risks, consequences of opting for no active treatment, effect on quality of life, coverage of treatment options and support for shared decision-making. The check list is intended for use by consumer health information providers to ensure that the information given to patients meets minimum standards, but it was not designed to be used to judge the scientific reliability of the information, nor whether it meets the varied needs of specific groups of patients.

Various criteria have been recommended for evaluating the quality of patient information (Entwistle *et al.* 1996b, Silberg *et al.* 1997, Wyatt 1997, Rippen 1997, Jadad and Gagliardi 1998). These include:

- accessibility;
- acceptability;
- readability and comprehensibility;
- style and attractiveness of presentation;
- accuracy and reliability of the content;
- coverage and comprehensiveness;
- currency and arrangements for editorial review;
- reference to sources and strength of evidence;
- where to find further information;
- credibility of authors, publishers and sponsors;
- relevance and utility.

Despite the existence of a number of rating scales and quality checklists, there are few published examples of evaluations of patient information materials to see the extent to which they match up to these criteria. Our study attempted to remedy that gap by evaluating patient information materials currently in use in the UK, using qualitative data and a simple scoring system.

It is important that the information given is both scientifically justified (in accordance with available evidence) and presented in a form acceptable and useful to patients. Clinical research specialists, ideally informed by rigorous systematic reviews of relevant research, are best placed to assess the accuracy of information, but only patients can judge the acceptability and usefulness of materials intended for them. We therefore involved both patients and clinical research specialists in our investigation to find out if the available information met the highest standards of scientific reliability and acceptability to patients.

Chapter 4

Aims of the study

Our study focused on patients' views of their information needs and the relevance and reliability of materials, and on an independent assessment of the clinical content of the materials by academic specialists.

The study had four aims:

- to identify the factors which patients consider important in assessing the quality and usefulness of information materials;
- to identify the extent and nature of information materials available for patients with ten common health problems;
- to assess the quality of these materials, especially with respect to their evidence-based content and usefulness in promoting shared decision-making between patients and health professionals;
- to develop guidelines for the production of high quality patient information materials.

These aims were achieved by collecting relevant materials and organising reviews of these by groups of patients who had experienced one of the specific health problems and by clinical and academic specialists with relevant expertise in the topic, including familiarity with systematic reviews of research evidence.

Chapter 5

Methods

Choice of health problems

The development of methodologies for conducting systematic reviews of research evidence on clinical topics, and computer databases such as that developed by the Cochrane Collaboration, have greatly improved the accessibility of research knowledge (Chalmers *et al.* 1997). The Cochrane Library database, which includes the Database of Abstracts of Research Evidence (DARE) produced by the NHS Centre for Reviews and Dissemination, and the paper-based *Effective Health Care* bulletins, have brought together current best evidence on the effectiveness of clinical treatments, making it much more widely available than hitherto. These overviews provided the 'gold standard' against which to evaluate the scientific quality of information contained in materials designed for patients.

The choice of health problems for investigation was determined by the availability of systematic reviews of the research evidence at the time the study was planned. The main source was the *Effective Health Care* bulletins published by the NHS Centre for Reviews and Dissemination (CRD) at York University. The bulletins, which are designed for use by commissioners of health services, are based on systematic review and synthesis of research on the clinical effectiveness, cost-effectiveness and acceptability of health service interventions. The reviews are carried out by a research team using established methodological guidelines, with advice from expert consultants for each topic. Great care is taken to ensure that conclusions reached fairly and accurately summarise the research findings.

Nine of the ten conditions chosen for this study had been the subject of *Effective Health Care* bulletins. The remaining condition (back pain) had been extensively reviewed by the Clinical Standards Advisory Group (CSAG), a body set up in 1991 to provide advice to Health Ministers and the NHS on standards of clinical care. The ten health problems or treatments which were considered in our study were:

- back pain;
- cataract;
- depression;
- glue ear;
- high cholesterol;
- hip replacement;
- infertility;
- menorrhagia;
- prostate enlargement;
- stroke rehabilitation.

Identification and selection of materials

A number of information providers were contacted with a request to supply patient information materials on any of the above conditions. These included the following types of organisation:

- *Self-help groups and the voluntary sector:* Databases of health information materials developed by the Health Education Board for Scotland (HEBS) and the Help for Health Trust were searched to identify original materials and consumer groups providing materials.

- *Health authorities and trusts:* A request for patient information materials was sent to 64 NHS trusts and 32 health authorities or health boards in England, Scotland, Wales and Northern Ireland. The names were drawn from the *NHS Handbook* by selecting the organisations with the largest financial turnover. In each case the letter was addressed to the person responsible for patient information. In trusts this included the directors of nursing and quality, of patient services, of health promotion, or the *Patient's Charter* co-ordinator. In health authorities or boards the letter went to the director of public health or the director of health promotion.

- *Commercial sources:* Drug companies and other commercial organisations, including publishers, were contacted. Drugs used to treat any of the ten conditions were identified from the *British National Formulary* and 25 major drug companies manufacturing these products were approached. Other publishers of patient information were identified from the HEBS and Help for Health Trust databases and from personal contacts.

- *Professional organisations:* The medical and nursing royal colleges were contacted and other relevant professional bodies such as the Chartered Society of Physiotherapists.

- *Other:* Advertisements were placed in the *Health Service Journal* and *Quality in Health Care*.

Selecting materials for review

Since it was not feasible to organise reviews of all the materials sent, it was necessary to make a selection. Materials were deemed eligible for the study if they met the following criteria:

- they were relevant to one of the selected conditions or treatments;
- they referred to more than one treatment option;
- they included some reference to treatment outcomes.

Early on in the study it became apparent that it was inappropriate to ask reviewers to assess more than five materials on any one topic, so the total was restricted to five for all but two conditions.

Selection of materials was purposive in that we aimed to cover a range of different types of materials over the ten topics, including materials from different sources and basic leaflets as well as more detailed materials.

While all materials were intended to meet patients' information needs, few of them were explicitly aimed at promoting shared decision-making. Nevertheless, in providing information about treatment options, they had the potential to assist decision-making, albeit implicitly, and they were assessed with that in mind.

Publishers' questionnaire

A questionnaire was sent to the publishers of each of the materials selected for assessment to obtain further information about how the materials were produced and the purposes for which they were intended (see Appendix). The questionnaire asked for information about the people responsible for writing and producing the material, any plans for revising it, the publisher's aims in producing it, the types of patients it was intended for, the means of distribution, the production process, involvement of patients or clinical experts in the production, and whether it had been evaluated.

Recruitment of patients and organisation of focus groups

One focus group was organised for each health problem or treatment. Patients were recruited to participate in the study by various means. Members of various patient groups were circulated with an invitation to assist in the study (the Prostate Help Association, the Stroke Association, OpenMind, Women's Health); advertisements were placed in newspapers and magazines (*Daily Mail* (see box), *The Voice, Health Which?, Women's Realm, Women's Own, Western Daily Press, King's Fund SHARE Newsletter*), clinicians were asked to recruit patients, and personal contacts were also used.

HELP WANTED: The King's Fund, an independent health charity, is appealing for volunteers to give their opinion on the content, usefulness and presentation of information materials. Ten conditions are under study: back pain, cataracts, cholesterol, depression, glue ear, hip replacement, menorrhagia, stroke, sub-fertility and prostatic hyperplasia. Findings will be published in 1997. For details call MICE on 0171-307 2671.

Source: Daily Mail, Monday 30 September 1996

Much of the recruitment to focus groups was done via newspaper advertisements, and some was done via self-help groups. For some conditions (e.g. back pain, depression), relatively high response rates were obtained and the project team used filter questions to select participants with a range of ages, social backgrounds, length of experience of the condition and treatments received. For other conditions (e.g. infertility, menorrhagia), recruitment to the focus groups was more difficult.

People responding to the initial invitations were sent a screening questionnaire, and if they were found to be eligible (i.e. they had recent experience of the relevant health problem – or in the case of glue ear, were parents of children who had had this problem) and were willing to participate, they were invited to join one of the focus groups.

Focus group participants

In total 62 patients participated in the focus groups. Nine of these were held in London and one in York (Table 1).

Table 1 Focus groups: participants and dates

Back pain	9 participants (2 men, 7 women)	Nov 1996
Cataract	5 participants (2 men, 3 women)	Mar 1997
Depression	8 participants (2 men, 6 women)	Oct 1996
Glue ear	4 participants (all mothers)	Jan 1997
High cholesterol	6 participants (3 men, 3 women)	Nov 1996
Hip replacement	7 participants (1 man, 6 women)	Feb 1997
Infertility	4 participants (all women)	Mar 1997
Menorrhagia	5 participants (all women)	Jan 1997
Prostate	8 participants (all men)	Dec 1996
Stroke	6 participants (2 men, 4 women)	Feb 1997

Materials were sent out to participants a few days before the focus groups were held. Participants were asked to give each of the materials a rating out of ten, and to note down what they liked and disliked about them. They were asked to bring these score sheets with them to the focus group meetings.

Focus groups were facilitated by expert facilitators from Social and Community Planning and Research (SCPR) (four groups) and by the study researcher, who received training at SCPR (six groups). The duration of the focus group meetings was between one and a half and two hours.

A topic guide was developed to assist the facilitators to structure the discussion and to ensure some uniformity across the groups (see Appendix). This covered introductory remarks; background information about participants; their experience of the health problem; their experience of using information materials and involvement in treatment decisions; their information needs; and their reactions to the specific information materials, including the presentation, style and tone of the materials, their credibility and usefulness in assisting decision-making. If time allowed, participants were asked to indicate which materials they liked best and which least, and to re-rate the materials in the light of the discussion. In some cases, groups went on to discuss their general views on different types of media, i.e. written materials versus audio or video.

People who are members of self-help groups or respond to advertisements are likely to be more interested in their medical problem and may have had greater exposure to information about the condition and its treatment than those who have not. It is likely therefore that our sample of focus group participants is skewed towards the 'better informed' end of the broader populations of people with the conditions studied. Although each focus group comprised people with experience of a particular condition, there was a good deal of variation within groups in terms of the precise nature, severity and duration of the problems that people experienced, and of the treatments they had been offered and given for the condition. In all groups, both positive and negative experiences of care were reported.

Analysis of data from focus groups

The focus group discussions were audiotaped and transcribed. In one group the tape recorder failed to record during part of the discussion, so notes of key points were made during and immediately after the discussions by the facilitator. Both transcripts and notes were used in the analysis.

Several main topic areas had been previously identified as of interest, as reflected in the topic guide. These included:

- experiences of communication, information provision and involvement during episodes of care;
- information seeking behaviours;
- views about information and involvement in decision-making;
- features of content and presentation that were liked and disliked in patient information materials.

The *Framework* approach (Richie and Spencer 1994) was used for the analysis of qualitative data from the focus group, although the indexing stage was omitted. The first stage of the analysis involved reading and becoming familiar with the contents of the focus group transcripts. Themes emerging from the transcripts were then identified and charted. Charting involves recording summaries of pertinent discussion points in large grids, the columns of which represent topic themes and the rows of which represent the people who made the points. Two sets of charts were constructed independently by two of the researchers. The first produced a set of charts for each focus group, with rows representing individual members of the groups. The second produced a set of charts with each row representing a single focus group.

Working through the columns of each chart, the range of experiences described and views expressed on particular topic themes were readily identified. These were summarised in prose. The two approaches to charting the material resulted in a consistent identification of points.

The focus group approach was not designed to produce a set of views that could be said to be statistically representative of the views of the population as a whole. We were looking to identify a range of experiences and views from people with a variety of health conditions. The summary of the findings from the focus group discussions identifies experiences which recurred across groups, points on which there was striking agreement among participants across groups, points on which there were divergences of opinion among participants, and themes which were specific to one or more of the health problems considered. Patients' comments about particular materials are summarised in the individual material review reports (Part 2).

Recruitment of academic specialists and organisation of reviews

Three clinical or academic specialists were recruited for each topic. Specialist reviewers had expert knowledge of the subject and were familiar with the relevant systematic reviews. Most had been involved in the development of the *Effective Health Care* bulletins or had been responsible for related research into treatment efficacy. All reviewers also had an interest in patient information and a few of them had experience of developing patient information materials.

A checklist to assess the quality of the materials and their scientific accuracy and completeness was developed, piloted and refined (see Appendix). Specialist reviewers were asked to give their assessments of each of the information materials in relation to general information about the condition and its causes and consequences, coverage of diagnostic interventions and treatment options, information about self-care and lifestyle changes, about uncertainties or knowledge gaps, the general balance or bias of the information provided, comprehensibility and readability, style and tone, explanations of technical terms, visual appeal, and the extent to which it provided patients with the information they needed to participate in decisions about treatment. Reviewers were asked to give an overall rating summarising their views of the material (out of ten) and ratings for each of the specific characteristics listed above (out of five).

In addition to completing the quantitative assessments of each characteristic of the materials, reviewers provided written comments in response to the specific questions. These have been summarised in the individual material review reports (Part 2).

Chapter 6

Patients' views on information and involvement

Experience of involvement in treatment decisions

It was a recurring theme across the focus groups that many of the participants did not feel that they had been offered any choices about their treatment by health professionals. Typically they reported having been told what doctors wanted to do to (or for) them, so their only implied choice was between whether or not to accept what was proposed. Some people had not realised when their treatment decisions were made that there were other options, and several only came to hear of particular treatment options via the information materials they were sent during the course of this project.

There was much sympathy for the constraints under which practitioners had to work, but comments made in several groups suggested that people thought that health professionals (particularly general practitioners) whom they encountered had not been aware of all the treatment options. This was particularly the case for treatment options delivered by different types of health professionals (e.g. osteopathy), and for relatively new techniques (e.g. phakoemulsification in cataract surgery). Other perceived reasons for health professionals not offering options were that they simply did not consider any other options, that they were personally unable to deliver them, or that they were constrained by limited budgets.

> 'My experience has been that if I've wanted information I've had to find it myself. It's not been offered. I've had to always struggle to find out information.
>
> Woman with fertility problems

Some people had found out about treatment options from the media, libraries, or other patients, and had then gone on to seek out the interventions they wanted. A few had turned to the private sector in order to be able to choose a particular surgeon and/or intervention. In all focus groups there were people who reported having to take the initiative and be assertive in order to obtain the forms of care they felt they needed. They described having to 'push', 'pester' or 'fight' to get general practitioners to take the problems of menorrhagia seriously, for example, or to get stroke after-care, counselling for depression, or a hip replacement.

Although some participants were quite adamant that they should be the ones to make the final decisions about their treatment, others were less confident about their ability to do this and more comfortable with a model in which a 'good' health professional whom they trusted made the decisions. There were several suggestions in the focus group discussions that people would have felt more involved in their care if they had been better informed, even if they had not played an active role in making the decision about which treatment they would have, as the quotation below illustrates.

> *'I expect them to say, "Well this is the avenue we should be going down now" but I don't want to just sit there and say, "Well yes, that's fine". I want to know as much as I can about what they're going to do, as much as I can understand. So if every time I came up [to the clinic] I came away with a big pile of leaflets, I'd be quite happy … I'd think I'd be getting somewhere and I'm involved in this. And, as I say, although you're not able to say, "Well, we'll try that one rather than that one, I think that sounds more the way I'd like to go". Even if you don't have that choice – at least you know why you're having whatever you're having, what you can expect to happen, which often they don't tell you. The girls were saying earlier about the side-effects – they don't tell you things like that.'*

Woman with fertility problems

Information provision by health professionals

Within all groups a few positive experiences of good communication with health professionals were reported. These were overshadowed, however, by substantial dissatisfaction with communication with health professionals. The overwhelming majority of focus group participants had wanted much more information about their condition and treatment than they were given. The statements below summarise experiences that were described repeatedly across all the focus groups:

- As patients, you are not offered information, verbal or written.

- If you want information, you have to ask for it, and you feel as though you are being a nuisance in doing so. (And some doctors actively discourage questions.)
- Even when you are aware of your information needs, it is often very difficult to get appropriate information in time to allow you to prepare for consultations, think about options, and prepare for treatment.
- Health professionals vary in their willingness to provide information, even when asked.
- Very little written information is provided about treatments.

The implications of not being adequately informed about treatment options were recognised to be serious. Several people suggested they would have thought differently about accepting particular treatments if they had been better informed about them.

Focus group participants offered several reasons for the inadequacy of information provision by health professionals. These included:

- *'System' problems:* People were aware that doctors are often very busy and do not seem to have time to explain or discuss things.

- *'Attitude' problems:* There was a view that many health professionals assume that patients do not want (or cannot cope with) information. However, focus group participants also thought that not all patients would want as much information as they had wanted. The perception that health professionals did not take their particular problems seriously was quite common among focus group participants, especially those with prostate enlargement, high cholesterol levels and heart disease, menorrhagia and sub-fertility.

- *'Knowledge' problems:* Several participants expressed concern that general practitioners were not aware of all the treatment options relevant to their condition, or did not know about the outcomes (particularly side-effects) of certain interventions. During discussions about information needs, the need for information to 'educate' general practitioners about a condition and/or possible treatments was identified in several of the focus groups.

Information from other sources

The people who participated in the focus groups had obtained information about their condition and its treatment from a variety of sources, most commonly the news media (television and newspapers), magazines, and voluntary organisations and self-help groups. They all appeared receptive to any relevant information they might chance across, and quite a few mentioned having actively sought out information from public libraries, friends or acquaintances who were health professionals, and other patients or people who might have experience of the problem.

> 'I did feel fairly well informed, but only because I'd deliberately sought out information, you know. I mean I hadn't actually been given any information by my GP or by the consultant at the hospital. So by my own efforts I felt quite well informed.'
>
> Woman with menorrhagia

Information chanced across in the media had prompted several people to initiate discussions with health professionals about their treatment as they became aware of possible side-effects, or of treatments with more attractive benefit/risk profiles. However, information presented in the media was not always well tailored to their particular information needs. Finding information to answer the *specific* questions they asked was frequently reported to be difficult. Several people reported being unable to obtain information using public libraries or 'scaring [themselves] to death' or 'getting out of [their] depth' with medical reference books. People seemed aware that information sources varied in their reliability, but expressed some different ideas about which sources could be trusted and why.

Despite being relatively active information users and seekers, many of the participants had been positively surprised by the selection of information materials they were sent to review for this study, and had never realised so much information was produced for patients. This led some to think initially that all the leaflets they were sent were 'wonderful' (they were so much better than nothing), although they tended to become far more critical once they had read a few.

> 'I would have read this quite avidly if I'd had it when I was starting out because you hear so many bits that don't actually mean anything from the

medical people themselves. I would have picked this up. No it's not attractive,
it's not got nice pictures on it, but it tells you something.'

Person with back pain

There was widespread support for the idea that this information should be made available by their health care providers. A wish was also expressed for 'a central point that had all the information that you need'.

Types of information wanted

People identified a wide range of information requirements and had some quite clear ideas about the kinds of information that were needed at particular times during the course of illness and treatment. Although there were differences in emphasis between the focus groups that reflected the particular problems experienced by people with different conditions, there were a lot of common themes. Broadly speaking, people wanted information for the following reasons:

- **To explain what is wrong:** People reported needing information to help them understand what had happened to them (especially, for example, for people recovering from a stroke or heart attack), what had 'gone wrong' and what was causing their symptoms. For some people, this information would be useful once they had recovered to help them make sense of their illness. For example, information about depression could allow people to 'see what [they] have been through'.

- **To gain a realistic idea of prognosis:** People appreciated hopeful but honest answers to the question of 'What does the future hold for me?'

- **To make the most of consultations:** Before consultations, people appreciated information that helped them identify questions that they needed to ask health professionals during consultations. They also liked materials that helped them to describe their symptoms clearly and accurately to health professionals. After consultations, people wanted information that would help them to remember what had been said, and possibly to answer questions that they had not thought of during the consultation.

'If given this then you could pursue it with the consultant and say, "Look,
it says in here … what are the chances?" That's the value of this booklet –

it gives you a whole range of questions to ask. If you didn't know there were any side-effects you'd never ask.'

Man with prostate problem

- **To understand the processes and likely outcomes of possible tests and treatments:** This information was wanted to help people decide whether or not to accept the treatments proposed by health professionals; to help them understand how treatments worked; to let them know what to expect and enable them to prepare for treatment; to be aware of potential side-effects; and to ensure they obtained any necessary follow-up checks etc. Some people wanted this information to enable them to contribute to (or make) decisions about which treatments they wanted.

   'As I read through it my confidence grew and when I put it down I felt, "Oh, one can really do something about this ..." Having this information I'd be able to discuss it with my doctor or gynaecologist. I'd be able to say, "Well, what about this?" Shall we try ...?'

Woman with menorrhagia

- **To assist in self-care:** Information was wanted about how to look after oneself and how to self-treat if that was appropriate.

- **To learn about available services and sources of help:** People felt they needed to be better informed about the kind of help available to them, and from where and how they could get it. This was particularly important for people with chronic conditions and those likely to experience a period of rehabilitation, for example after a stroke or hip replacement operation.

- **To provide reassurance and help to cope:** Without wanting falsely optimistic information, people did appreciate information that let them know they were not alone in having the kinds of problems they were experiencing and that somebody understood what they were going through. Practical suggestions about how to cope and manage on a day to day basis were generally appreciated. Acknowledgement of the emotional difficulties that often accompany physical problems was particularly appreciated by members of the back pain, stroke and sub-fertility focus groups.

- **To help others understand:** In most groups, participants expressed a need for information about their condition for other people. Discussion of this often arose in the context of comments about how insensitive other people could be to their problems. Focus group participants wanted information for their families, friends, and sometimes employers and the 'general public' so that these people could better understand how the condition affected them and what adjustments they needed to make to their lives in order to manage or cope with the condition. Information for family members was thought particularly important for conditions that would have a major impact on other people's lives, including those that forced or warranted lifestyle changes. Information for the general public appeared to be particularly important for people who felt stigmatised by their condition (e.g. depression), and also by those who thought their condition was at least to some extent preventable (e.g. heart disease, depression).

> 'When my husband saw this video [sent to focus group participants for review] he watched it and said, "My God I wish this had been available, I would have understood. I understand now what you must have been going through." He just couldn't get it, you see, why I couldn't see the bird, 'cause the light was good, it wasn't dark ... When he saw the video and it simulated the effect of a cataract, how it just mists over and you can't see the eye chart or anything, he realised then why I couldn't see. If we could have had that out of a video library from the hospital we could have both watched it together. He would have been more able to help me.'
>
> Woman with cataract

- **To legitimise their help-seeking and concerns:** People who had felt that their problems were treated dismissively by health professionals and/or family and friends appreciated information materials that described their problems, acknowledged some of the difficulties they faced and suggested that professional help should be sought. A few also mentioned that written information about, for example, the side-effects of treatments, could be useful when dealing with health professionals who did not take their concerns about side-effects seriously.

- **To identify further information and self-help groups:** Suggestions for further reading, and more importantly contact details for self-help groups and organisations that could provide information and advice about a particular condition were universally welcomed. However, it was pointed out in several focus groups that contact details alone were of little use if people did not know what kind of information and services organisations could provide.

- *To identify the 'best' health care providers:* A few people mentioned the desire or possibility of choosing 'the best' health care providers. These tended to be people who were able to take advantage of private as well as national health services. The criteria they used to determine who was 'the best' were not explored.

Changing information needs

The theme of information needs changing over time recurred throughout the focus groups. People who had had strokes described wanting just enough information soon after their stroke to help them through the initial 'bewildered' phase. They needed to understand what had happened to them but did not want too much more information at that stage. Later on, they needed more detailed information about what had happened, together with good practical information about rehabilitation services and how to manage their daily lives.

During severe bouts of depression, people did not feel they wanted, or would be able to cope with, information about their condition and its treatment. When they were a little better, they might appreciate information presented on audio or videotape, which required less concentration than written materials.

People with chronic conditions often perceived themselves to have progressed beyond the need for 'introductory' information leaflets onto more comprehensive and detailed information sources. Many became 'experts' with very specific information needs.

People facing decisions that included some form of surgical option tended to want more detailed information about that option as it became a more likely choice. While it was a remote possibility, gory details were not appreciated.

Contested content areas

There were very few areas of information content about which focus group participants disagreed. The disagreements could often be summarised as being about when information was wanted or not, or 'where the balance lies', rather than about a type of information being viewed absolutely as desirable or not. Women with fertility problems were unsure about whether or not information leaflets should cover issues such as coming to terms with infertility and adoption. The focus group participants generally felt that they did not want to give up hope of having their own child, and that it would be a long time before they would want to read about these things.

The content area about which there was most disagreement was information about the side-effects and risks of treatments. Even in this area, however, there was agreement that people should be informed about the main known risks, and leaflets which failed to mention or downplayed important risks were generally criticised. The main arguments presented in favour of provision of information about risks were:

- if you don't know about risks or side-effects, you can't make informed decisions about treatments;
- it is better to inform people about possible risks before they happen.

Arguments put forward in favour of limiting the amount of information provided about risks, and doubts about the wisdom of providing all possible information about all possible risks included:

- a querying of the necessity of telling people about extremely rare risks;
- a concern that people might make decisions that are ultimately detrimental to their well-being if they are told about, and unduly influenced by, long lists of side-effects, the gory details of surgery and treatment risks;
- a concern that it can become very difficult for parents to consent to an operation for a child if the consultant spells out everything that could go wrong (glue ear);
- a view that information about risks should be presented together with information about benefits ('a pros and cons sheet, for and against').

The approach most likely to cater for all preferences was perhaps summed up by one participant who praised a leaflet that dealt adequately with the risks – it provided basic information about the main ones in such a way that it would be relatively easy to pursue further information as required.

It was clear that the way in which risk information is presented is important. Participants praised some leaflets for presenting information about risks in a positive and reassuring way and disliked others that presented risks in a negative and offputting way. Content and presentation issues thus cannot be seen as entirely separate matters. Some types of information are more acceptably presented in some ways than others.

Presentation issues

There was striking agreement across and within focus groups about several aspects of information presentation. These included: the tone/mood in which information is presented; the tone/stance adopted by the producer; the way the audience is addressed; the ease of access to information (the readability, structure and layout of leaflets, for example); the overall impression of production quality. The terms used by participants to describe what they liked and disliked about these aspects of presentation are listed in Table 2.

Table 2

	Liked	*Disliked*
Tone/mood	Positive, hopeful, encouraging, cheerful, optimistic, reassuring, constructive, non-alarmist	Negative, off-putting, stresses all the things which could go wrong, alarmist
Tone/stance	Honest, practical, down to earth, sympathetic, understanding, not condescending, doesn't talk down to you	Unrealistic, glosses over real problems, glosses over possible after effects, over-optimistic, misleading, disinterested, written by someone doing a job, patronising, talking down to me, childish, dismissive in tone, flippant, judgemental
Relating to the audience	Talks to you, relates to you personally, treats you as an individual, uses 'you' a lot, chatty, friendly, warm, womanly, human touch.	Talks about patients not people, clinical, impersonal, cold, distant, too formal, sterile, remote, dry, like a tax form.
Language/ readability	Clear, easy to read, easy to understand, plain speaking, simple, understandable language, straightforward wording, spells out the terms, puts more clinical words in brackets	Complicated language and explanation, too technical, badly written
Structure	Structured and concise, clear headings, sections allow you to dip in and out, succinct, important sections highlighted, short blocks of text, well indexed,	Jumbled up, slabs of text, dense text, too long
Layout	Large print, uncluttered, not filled with print, nice mix of drawings and print	Small typeface, hard to read, unattractive layout, boring presentation,
Overall impression of production	Professional looking production	Drab, cheap, amateurish, appearance of cost-cutting

Interactive elements of information materials

Participants responded enthusiastically to features in leaflets that actively engaged them while helping them to clarify their current situation and think about their preferences. These included: diary type charts on which to record symptoms (e.g. amount and duration of menstrual loss for menorrhagia); a checklist of activities that could be used to assess the extent to which a condition bothered them (cataract); questions to ask themselves before making a decision; and space to write down questions or points that they wanted to remember during consultations.

> 'I think the Buckinghamshire Health Authority [leaflet] does it very well – on page 4, "Should I have an operation?" and there on page 5 are at least about ten points where you can put yes, no, doesn't matter to me – and that I think would help a lot of patients.'
>
> Person with cataract

In several groups amusement and frustration were expressed at the suggestions made in leaflets that people should ask their doctors for particular types of information. Some participants were rather pessimistic about this, given their previous difficulties with extracting information from health professionals.

What good leaflets can do

Focus group participants described a range of occasions on which information had made a difference to how they behaved or felt and highlighted the potential benefits of information materials. Some of these benefits have already been alluded to in the section 'Types of information wanted' so they are listed only briefly here. Good information materials can:

Help people to help themselves by:

- coping with practical and emotional problems on a daily basis;
- self-treating where appropriate;
- seeking out effective forms of professional help or lay support;
- finding out more about their condition and treatment.

Help people to get more out of professional health care by:

- clearly explaining relevant symptoms and problems;

- asking the questions that are important to them;
- having appropriate expectations about the types of treatment and standard of care that should be offered;
- knowing they can accept or reject particular forms of care.

Make people feel better because they:

- know that their problems are real and recognised;
- know that they are not alone in having these problems;
- can identify ways of improving their situation or coping with it;
- feel more confident and in control.

Chapter 7

Availability of patient information materials

Materials obtained and selected for review

The survey of information providers elicited positive responses from 78 organisations which between them sent copies of 128 printed materials, eight audiotapes or telephone helplines and four videos.

The materials, which ranged from duplicated factsheets to professionally produced glossy publications, were developed and published by a variety of different types of organisation, including commercial publishers, private health care organisations, consumer groups and voluntary organisations, drug and equipment manufacturers, NHS trusts and health authorities, professional and academic bodies. Some information producers sent materials on more than one topic.

Samples of patient information materials were obtained from the following organisations (Box 4):

BOX 4 INFORMATION MATERIALS OBTAINED

Commercial publishers/private health care:
Butterworth-Heinemann (back pain)
EMIS (cataract, glue ear*, infertility, stroke rehabilitation)
Fish Foundation (high cholesterol)
General Practitioner (menorrhagia)
Hadley Hutt Computing (infertility)
Hawler Publications (depression*)
Krames Communications (depression*, high cholesterol, hip replacement, infertility, menorrhagia*)
PatientWise (back pain*, high cholesterol*, prostate enlargement*)
Pritchett & Hull (hip replacement, stroke rehabilitation)
PPP Healthcare (cataract, hip replacement*, infertility*)
Scriptographic (back pain, depression*, prostate enlargement*)
Videos for Patients (depression*, prostate enlargement*)

contd.

Box 4 *contd.*

Consumer groups/voluntary organisations:
Arthritis Care (hip replacement)
Australian Conductive Deafness Association (glue ear)
British Heart Foundation (high cholesterol)*
Chest, Heart and Stroke Association (stroke rehabilitation)*
College of Health (depression*, glue ear*, hip replacement, infertility, prostate
   enlargement*)
Depression Alliance (depression)
Family Heart Association (high cholesterol)
Mind (depression*)
National Deaf Children's Society (glue ear)
Royal National Institute for the Blind (cataract*)
Stroke Association (stroke rehabilitation*)
Women's Health (infertility*, menorrhagia*)
Women's Health Concern (infertility*, menorrhagia*)

Drug and equipment manufacturers:
Bencard (prostate enlargement)
Bridge Pharmaceuticals (prostate enlargement)
Ciba-Geigy (back pain)
Coloplast Foundation (prostate enlargement)
Crookes Healthcare (back pain*)
DePuy (hip replacement*)
Duphar Laboratories (depression)
Invicta Pharmaceuticals (prostate enlargement*)
Johnson & Johnson (hip replacement)
Merck, Sharpe & Dohme (high cholesterol*, prostate enlargement)
Pharmaceutical Division, 3M Health Care (back pain)
Richborough Pharmaceuticals (glue ear)
Serono Laboratories (infertility*)
Smith & Nephew (prostate enlargement)
SmithKline Beecham (depression*)
Tambrands (menorrhagia)
Zeneca Pharmaceuticals (glue ear)

NHS organisations:
Bedfordshire Health Authority (glue ear*)
Blackburn, Hyndburn and Ribble Valley NHS Trust (hip replacement)
Buckinghamshire Health Authority (cataract*)
Central Sheffield University Hospitals (infertility, menorrhagia*, prostate enlargement)
East Lancashire Health Authority (back pain*)
Gloucester Day Case Cataract Unit (cataract*)
Health Promotion Wales (high cholesterol*)
Hertfordshire Health Authorities (glue ear*)

contd.

Box 4 *contd.*
North Ayrshire and Arran NHS Trust (infertility)
Plymouth Community Services NHS Trust (prostate enlargement)
Portsmouth Health Care NHS Trust (stroke rehabilitation)
Royal Free Hospital, London (glue ear)
South Manchester University Hospitals NHS Trust (hip replacement, stroke
  rehabilitation*)
The Royal Hospitals, Belfast (cataract, hip replacement, infertility)
United Bristol Healthcare NHS Trust (cataract*)
University Hospital, Nottingham (menorrhagia)
Walsgrave Hospital, Coventry (cataract*, high cholesterol, prostate enlargement)
Whittington Hospital, London (back pain)

Professional/academic bodies:
Action Research (back pain)
American Academy of Family Physicians (high cholesterol)
Arthritis and Rheumatism Research Council (back pain, hip replacement*)
Association of Health Care Policy and Research, US Department of Health and
  Human Services (back pain, cataract, depression, stroke rehabilitation*)
British Medical Association (glue ear, high cholesterol*)
Chartered Society of Physiotherapists (back pain)
Hearing Research Trust (glue ear*)
Institute of Hearing Research (glue ear)
Nottingham University Research and Treatment Unit in Reproduction (infertility*)
Organisation of Chartered Physiotherapists in Private Practice (back pain)
Pain Research Institute (back pain)
Royal College of General Practitioners (depression)
Royal College of Obstetricians and Gynaecologists (menorrhagia*)
Royal College of Psychiatrists (depression*)
Royal College of Surgeons of England (hip replacement*, prostate enlargement*)
The Stationery Office (back pain*)

* materials reviewed

This list of materials covering just ten clinical conditions is impressively long, but it would be misleading to conclude that patients with these conditions have ready access to information. Distribution of patient information materials continues to be problematic. Most of the focus group participants said they had experienced great difficulty in getting hold of any printed or other information and many said they had been offered nothing at all. Development and acquisition of patient information materials is ad hoc and often dependent on the enthusiasm of individual clinicians. Distribution is often untargeted, leaflets being left in piles in the waiting room instead of being handed to patients when they consult. Many hospitals and general practices have no specific policy on the provision of patient information materials and no one with responsibility for ensuring that they are available and are provided to patients when they need them.

Table 3 Number of materials obtained and selected for review*

	Obtained	Reviewed
Back pain	20 printed	5 printed
Cataract	7 printed	3 printed
	1 video	1 video
	1 audio	1 audio
Depression	22 printed	6 printed
	1 video	1 video
	2 audio	1 audio
Glue ear	11 printed	4 printed
	1 audio	1 audio
High cholesterol	15 printed	5 printed
Hip replacement	13 printed	4 printed
	1 audio	1 audio
Infertility	12 printed	5 printed
	1 audio	
Menorrhagia	8 printed	5 printed
Prostate enlargement	13 printed	4 printed
	1 video	1 video
	1 audio	1 audio
Stroke	7 printed	3 printed
	1 video	1 video
	1 audio	1 audio

*Packs of factsheets or videos and audiotapes with accompanying printed material have been counted as one

Of the clinical topics covered in the survey, depression and back pain elicited the largest number of materials, with 25 and 20 respectively, whereas only nine each were obtained for menorrhagia and stroke rehabilitation. Fifty-four materials (42 per cent of the total) were selected for review (Table 3). (See p.20 for description of the selection criteria).

Survey of publishers of materials selected for review

Completed questionnaires were received from the publishers of 26 of the materials (48 per cent). While few of the materials included explicit statements of their aims and who they were intended for, responses to the questionnaire made it clear that the materials had been produced for a number of different purposes. Most of the information packages had been written by clinical experts and were intended to provide background information on the condition and its treatment for patients and their carers. In addition to providing an introduction to the topic, some publishers reported specific intentions, for example:

- *to promote self-care and prevent recurrence* (e.g. the information on back pain published by East Lancashire Health Authority and by the Stationery Office);

- *to raise awareness of a problem and encourage people to seek medical help* (e.g. the booklet on depression produced by the Royal College of Psychiatrists);

- *to prepare patients for specific treatments or surgical procedures* (e.g. the materials produced by Gloucester Day Case Cataract Unit, United Bristol Healthcare Trust, the Royal College of Surgeons, and Nottingham University infertility clinic).

- *to support informed treatment choice* (e.g. Bedfordshire Health Authority's glue ear leaflet and Buckinghamshire Health Authority's leaflet on cataract).

All but four of the publishers who returned the questionnaire claimed to have involved patients or potential users in the development of the materials. In a few cases this involved organising focus groups to discuss patients' information needs, but for the most part they had asked lay readers or consumer group representatives to comment on the design and content of the materials. Few publishers had used formal tests of readability (e.g. Gunning Fog Index) in developing the text. Only one publisher, Gloucester Day Case Cataract Unit, had plans to produce versions in other languages (Hindi and Urdu). In some cases a wide range of professional opinion had been canvassed, but for the most part publishers had relied on the expertise of the authors.

Most publishers were vague about the sources of evidence from which the information was drawn. Only two of the materials were explicitly based on systematic reviews of research into treatment efficacy (the leaflets produced by Bedfordshire and Buckinghamshire Health Authorities with the NHS Centre for Reviews and Dissemination).

Formal evaluation involving patients had been carried out or was planned for thirteen of the materials. The remainder had been evaluated informally or not at all. Most of the publishers who responded to the questionnaire had plans for updating the materials, but only Scriptographic, Emis and College of Health had systems for periodic review on a regular basis.

Chapter 8

Quality of patient information materials

Reviews by academic specialists and patients

Reviews were completed by 28 of the 30 academic specialists recruited. Two specialists who had originally agreed to assess the materials on infertility failed to return their assessments despite repeated reminders. All the remaining specialists completed the check lists and scoring sheets most conscientiously, providing detailed written comments, many of which have been included in Part 2 of this report.

The focus group participants were also asked to rate the overall quality of the materials and to bring written comments to the meeting, where each of the materials was then discussed. Comments of participants have been used to illustrate the reviews in Part 2.

Both focus group participants and academic specialists reported some difficulties in comparing the different materials, since it was obvious that they had different aims and scope. For example, some were designed to provide only a basic introduction to the topic, whereas others had more ambitious objectives and were designed for readers who wanted much greater detail. In general, reviewers were more enthusiastic about those that provided detailed information, the simpler leaflets being seen as too basic to be really useful.

Summary ratings

Patients and specialists were asked to rate each of the materials out of ten. Patients tended to be more generous in their ratings than specialists. Table 4 shows the number and proportion of materials which received high ratings (a mean score of eight or more out of ten) from patients and specialists.

Table 4 Number of materials receiving high ratings from patients and specialists

	Patients	Specialists
Back pain (n=5)	1	1
Cataract (n=5)	2	–
Depression (n=8)	4	1
Glue ear (n=5)	1	1
High cholesterol (n=5)	2	1
Hip replacement (n=5)	2	1
Infertility (n=5)	3	–
Menorrhagia (n=5)	1	–
Prostate (n=6)	3	1
Stroke (n=5)	3	–
Total (n=54)	22 (41%)	6 (11%)

Patients and specialists did not always agree and in some cases the materials were ranked quite differently by the two groups. For example, participants in the patient focus group on depression gave high ratings (mean 8.4) to the Mind publication *Making Sense of Treatment and Drugs – Anti-depressants*, whereas the specialists gave it the lowest rating out of the eight materials reviewed (mean 4.0). The patients liked the fact that the booklet provided detailed information about the pros and cons of different drugs, whereas the specialists felt the information it contained was biased and unbalanced, putting too much emphasis on the 'dangerousness' of drug treatments (see pp. 98–100).

Strong criticisms were levelled by specialists at another leaflet which was favourably rated by patients. The leaflet on stroke produced by South Manchester University Hospital was given top ranking in its group by focus group participants, achieving a mean score of 8.3, but the specialists gave it the lowest ranking and a mean score of 3.3. Focus group participants liked the fact that it provided information which would be useful to carers of people who had suffered strokes and they liked the emphasis on rehabilitation and the clear helpful diagrams, but the specialists pointed out that the leaflet contained many omissions, typographical mistakes and errors. They criticised the booklet for being out of date, anecdotal and not evidence-based (see pp. 185–187).

Discrepancies were also seen in the ratings given by specialists and patients to the booklet on hip replacement produced by DePuy International (pp. 135–136), and the Women's Health Concern (pp.142–144) and Serono

Laboratories (pp. 144–146) booklets on infertility. All of these were given favourable ratings by members of the patient focus groups, but the specialists felt they contained inaccurate, out-of-date and misleading information.

The leaflet on cholesterol checks produced by Merck, Sharp and Dohme was highly rated by the focus group (mean score 8.4) who were convinced about the value of cholesterol testing and liked the fact that it was attractive, well laid out and easy to read. The subject specialists, who were much less enthusiastic about cholesterol testing, gave this booklet a low rating (mean score 3.7). They criticised it for failing to explain the small contribution of cholesterol to total coronary heart disease risk and felt it would lead to some people being screened inappropriately (pp. 120–122).

In the case of *The Back Book*, published by the Stationery Office, the specialists were more enthusiastic than the patients, who gave it a score of 6.9 as compared to the specialists' mean score of 8.0. The messages in this booklet were broadly in tune with the specialists' view of the evidence on the efficacy of treatments for back pain, but conflicted with the personal experience of some of the focus group members who doubted its accuracy and disliked its tone (pp. 70–72).

Only four materials received high ratings (mean scores of 8 or more) from both patients and specialists. These were:

- Bedfordshire Health Authority's leaflet on glue ear;
- British Medical Association's Family Doctor booklet on high cholesterol;
- Royal College of Surgeons' booklet on hip replacement;
- Royal College of Surgeons' booklet on prostate surgery.

A further 20 materials received above average scores (6 or more) from both sets of reviewers, but were criticised for specific flaws:

- AHCPR booklet on back pain;
- Stationery Office booklet on back pain;
- Buckinghamshire Health Authority's leaflet on cataract;
- United Bristol Healthcare NHS Trust video on cataract;
- Royal College of Psychiatrists' booklet on depression;
- Hawker Publications leaflet on depression;
- Scriptographic booklet on depression;
- Videos for Patients video on depression;

- Institute of Hearing Research leaflet on glue ear;
- Hertfordshire Health Authorities' leaflet on glue ear;
- Health Promotion Wales leaflet on high cholesterol;
- College of Health telephone helpline on hip replacement;
- NURTURE information pack on infertility;
- Jessop Hospital leaflet on menorrhagia;
- Royal College of Obstetricians and Gynaecologists' booklet on menorrhagia;
- Women's Health leaflet on menorrhagia;
- Scriptographic booklet on prostate enlargement;
- Videos for Patients video on prostate enlargement;
- Stroke Association booklet on stroke;
- AHCPR booklet on stroke.

Specialists' ratings of specific aspects of the materials

In addition to the overall ratings that patients and specialists were asked to give to each of the materials, specialists rated particular characteristics of the materials by giving them a score out of 5. The mean scores are presented in Table 5.

Table 5   Specialists' ratings of specific characteristics of the materials

	Mean score (out of 5)
Style and readability	
Comprehensibility and readability	3.7
Style and tone	3.5
Explaining technical terms	3.3
Visual appeal	3.2
The condition	
General information about condition	3.3
Information about causes	2.8
Information about consequences	2.9
Treatment options	
Lifestyle changes, coping strategies or self-care	2.7
Uncertainties or gaps in knowledge	2.2
Balanced view of treatment options	2.5
Information to make informed choices	2.4

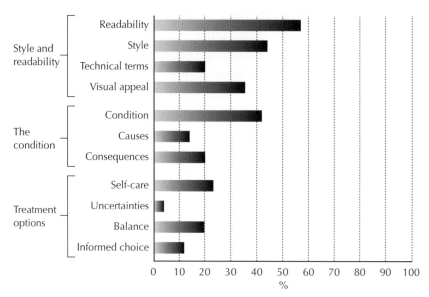

Figure 2 Specialists' ratings of specific characteristic the materials: percent scoring 4+

In general the materials received higher scores for presentation than for content. Figure 2 shows the number of materials that achieved high ratings (mean of 4 or more) for each dimension.

While more than half of the materials were given high ratings for readability, very few received high ratings for information about the causes and consequences of the condition and about treatment options. Only six of the 54 materials received above average ratings for promoting informed choice and only two were considered to be adequate in their coverage of uncertainties or knowledge gaps.

Overview of reactions to the materials

Acceptability: Most of the focus group participants were avid information seekers and their initial response to the materials they were sent for review was enthusiastic. On closer examination, however, they became more critical, but all remained positive about the general idea of information to support discussion about treatment options with health professionals.

Focus groups participants were not always unanimous in their reactions to the materials, underlining the fact that patients' information preferences are variable. This suggests a need for information packages in different formats to meet the needs of specific groups.

Media: Focus group participants and subject specialists were in general more concerned about the content and style of the materials than the medium. The information in printed materials could be easily referred to and shared with partners or carers. Audiotape or telephone helplines provided useful introductions to the subject and were particularly useful for people whose vision was impaired, e.g. those with cataract, but the helplines were often difficult to hear. Videos offered the possibility of including interviews with patients who had experienced the condition or treatment, which the focus group participants appreciated.

Tone: Perceptions of the tone of the materials affected patients' reactions to them. Several were criticised as being patronising, victim-blaming, dismissive, or promoting a 'doctor knows best' attitude. Participants and subject specialists gave low ratings to materials that were considered too prescriptive. A facilitative style was preferred.

> '*It's patronising – are they speaking to a child? It's verbose without imparting information. I hate this, the tone of it.*'
>
> Person who had a hip replacement

Readability and comprehensibility: Although most materials scored reasonably high marks for readability and comprehensibility, there were a number of examples where reviewers considered the print was too small or too dense to be inviting. Technical terms and medical diagnoses were sometimes included without explanation, for example, one leaflet about high cholesterol mentioned 'angina' without explaining what it means.

> "*It is best to avoid bending the leg up beyond 90° to the body. This is particularly so if the operation has involved a posterior approach to the joint.*"
> (*Arthritis and Rheumatism Council leaflet on hip replacement*)

> '*I don't know whether they'd given me a posterior approach!*'
>
> Person who had a hip replacement

Style and attractiveness of presentation: In general the use of pictures and diagrams was appreciated. Printed materials which did not include illustrations were considered boring. However, some patients were antagonistic to the use of certain illustrations. For example, in some cases cartoons were seen as 'trivialising' and not appropriate to the seriousness of the problem, e.g. depression. Sometimes inappropriate illustrations were used which gave a misleading impression of the problem, for example, the use of a bicycle chain to illustrate the spine in a book about back pain. 'Gory' or 'scary' pictures were not appreciated by patients.

The use of yellow paper and large sans serif print in materials on cataract was commended. One or two leaflets contained spelling mistakes, which were noted disapprovingly by both patients and specialists.

Accuracy and reliability of the content: In some ways this was the most worrying aspect of the materials we reviewed. Many contained inaccuracies and misleading statements which were picked up by the specialist reviewers. The most common fault was to give an over-optimistic view of the treatments, emphasising benefits and glossing over the risks and likely side-effects. The assumption on the part of many information producers that patients do not want to know about side-effects was not borne out by the views expressed in the focus groups. Most participants were adamant that they did want to know the full picture, as long as it was presented in a non-alarmist fashion.

While many materials contained reasonably clear descriptions of the disease or problem and common symptoms, the causes and consequences of the condition were much less well covered. This was a serious omission because focus group participants were clear that they, and people like them, needed to understand the natural history of the condition from which they were suffering in order to help them cope with it. Quantitative information about prevalence, recovery time and outcome probabilities was also absent from the majority of the materials reviewed. Again, these were topics which patients indicated they would like to know about.

Coverage and comprehensiveness: There is a fine balance between providing too little information in a leaflet, and too much. Many leaflets were considered too introductory and basic to be helpful, but a few contained too much technical detail, which reviewers considered impersonal and unnecessary.

Very few of the materials were considered to be of sufficient standard to support involvement in treatment decisions. They were not comprehensive in their coverage of the treatment options and the likely outcomes. In order to support shared decision-making, materials should include balanced information about risks and benefits and be honest about uncertainties and knowledge gaps. Most materials failed to provide information about outcome probabilities.

Patients also wanted to be told about things they could do themselves to manage the problem or to avoid risks, and they wanted information about the full range of treatment possibilities including complementary therapies or counselling.

Some otherwise good quality materials failed to provide information about treatments or management strategies which were not supported by evidence of efficacy. This was confusing for patients who had heard about these treatments and were keen to learn more. Instead of omitting information about such treatments, producers should include these in the information package together with an honest assessment of whether or not they are known to be effective. An evidence-based approach is essential in developing good quality patient information, but this does not mean that lack of evidence justifies the omission of mention of common treatments or possible outcomes. In the real world of clinical practice decisions often have to be made on the basis of incomplete evidence.

Currency and arrangements for editorial review: Nearly a third of the materials did not include a publication date, so it was not possible for readers to judge whether or not they were likely to contain out-of-date information. Some of the materials had been in circulation for many years without any attempt to review or update them. Specialist reviewers pointed out that many were indeed out of date, failing to include information about new treatments or recent research evidence.

The development of patient information materials cannot be seen as a one-off exercise. It requires a long term commitment to produce regular updates and to withdraw out-of-date materials from circulation. Materials should include an indication of their 'shelf life', beyond which date readers should be warned to seek alternative sources of information.

Reference to sources and strength of evidence: Very few of the materials contained any information about the primary sources on which they were based. It was rare for them to make any attempt to discuss the strength of research evidence for claims made. While the average lay reader cannot be expected to be familiar with details of research methodologies, people do want to be able to distinguish between well established facts and much weaker evidence or opinion.

Where to find further information: Quite a few of the materials contained details of additional sources of information or contact details for consumer and self-help groups. Some leaflets were intended primarily as an advertising vehicle for a particular organisation or product, in which case the further information sources were limited to the address and phone number of the producer of the leaflet. Occasionally, a range of contacts was suggested but without explanation of what they could provide. One leaflet on back pain gave the address of the National Association for Chiropractic but did not include any explanation of what chiropractic was, or its relevance to the treatment of back pain.

Credibility: Many materials failed to provide information about authorship or sponsorship, leaving readers in the dark about the credibility of the sources. Patients tended to be suspicious of leaflets which had an obvious commercial motive, for example those produced by drug companies or private health insurers, and there was some distrust of materials produced by NHS and government sources as well because of a perception that: 'They're out to save money.' Information produced by professional bodies or national associations such as the royal colleges or the British Heart Association inspired confidence. Some leaflets were thinly disguised sales brochures or publicity vehicles, including some of those produced by consumer organisations, and these were felt to be biased and therefore unreliable.

Relevance and utility: Patients' information requirements may change over the course of a disease. For example, at the time of first onset or diagnosis, it may be more relevant to provide details of the tests and investigations used and descriptive information about the condition and prognosis. Depending on the condition, it may be appropriate to provide detailed information about treatments at a later stage. On the other hand, many patients in the focus groups said they had wanted information at a much earlier stage than it was normally provided. Information about the consequences of surgery is more useful before the decision to undergo surgery is taken, but it is often not provided until the admission date has been agreed. Although some participants stated a preference for information 'a little at a time', others wanted more detailed booklets given early on as a reference source they could return to.

> *'I like the fact that it's in sections, which are coloured, so you can dip into it, depending upon which stage you're at. So if you're about to have the operation you'll be further along, if you've just been diagnosed you'll be at the beginning*

or whatever, but you can immediately go to the section you want. There's even a consent form in the middle.'

Person who had a hip replacement

Few of the materials reviewed were clearly aimed at promoting shared decision-making between professionals and patients. Focus group participants were particularly enthusiastic about materials which gave them a sense of empowerment. For example, those which reassured them that they were not alone in experiencing the symptoms, those that gave them ideas for self-help, and those which suggested questions they could ask the doctor. Checklists or blank pages to note down particular points for further consideration or discussion were appreciated.

'The back [of the leaflet] was helpful. You've got a lot of space that you can jot down questions to ask the doctor when you get there. I think it saves the doctor's time and your time and you don't forget anything.'

Parent of child with glue ear

Few of the developers had involved patients in all stages of the development of the materials and many materials appeared not to have been peer reviewed or tested with patients prior to distribution. This undoubtedly contributed to the poor quality of many of the information packages.

Chapter 9

Recommendations

Access to appropriate information can empower patients to express their treatment preferences and help professionals to improve the information base of clinical decisions. But if shared decision-making is to become a reality in the NHS, it will be necessary to develop the following resources:

- a supply of information materials for patients about treatment choices and outcomes based on scientifically valid systematic reviews of the research evidence;
- a system for assessing the quality of the information materials before they are promulgated to patients;
- a means by which health authorities, provider units, clinicians, consumer health information services and consumer groups can access the materials and make them available to patients;
- training programmes for clinicians and other information providers to help them elicit patients' preferences and use patient information materials effectively;
- a wide dissemination programme to tell patients about their rights to information and how to find it, and to encourage clinicians to provide it.

The establishment of the NHS-funded Centre for Health Information Quality, based in Winchester, is a good start.* The centre aims to act as a clearing house on all aspects of patient information and a centre of excellence on the creation of patient information, but the current level of short-term funding will not be sufficient to accomplish all the tasks listed above.

Developing high quality patient information is not a simple task. It requires collaborative efforts from people with a range of expertise, including health care professionals, patients, researchers, consumer health information specialists, journalists, designers and copy-editors (Entwistle *et al.* 1998). This study has revealed many deficiencies in the quality of patient information materials currently in use. We therefore recommend the adoption of the following guidelines for the production and use of patient information.

---

*For further information contact them at CHIQ, Highcroft, Romsey Road, Winchester SO22 5DH, tel: (01962) 863511 ext. 200, fax: (01962) 849079, email: enquiries@centreforhiq.demon.co.uk, Web site: http://www.centreforhiq.demon.co.uk.

Guidelines for the development of good quality patient information materials

The process

1. *Involve patients throughout the process:* Developers of patient information materials should start from an understanding of patients' information needs. These will vary for different conditions and treatments and may vary at different stages in a disease or course of treatment. The only way to find out what information patients need is to ask them. It is often a good idea to establish a focus group of patients with the same problem or condition or those who have experienced relevant treatments to discuss information needs. The same group could be asked to advise on design and content of materials.

2. *Involve a wide range of clinical experts:* During the course of a disease patients may come into contact with a range of health professionals, each of whom may bring a different approach to the problem. For example, consultants and hospital nurses may be particularly knowledgeable about specific treatment strategies, but GPs and community nurses may be more aware of the impact of the disease and treatment on patients' home lives. A surgeon is likely to prefer surgical treatments, a physiotherapist may be biased in favour of physical therapies, and so on. To ensure a balanced view all relevant clinicians should be asked to contribute, but ideally all should have knowledge of the research sources.

3. *Be specific about the purpose of the information and the target audience:* Very few of the materials we reviewed were explicit about who they were aimed at and what they hoped to achieve. Without this information it is difficult for users to judge whether their needs will be met and difficult for clinicians to select appropriate materials for their patients.

4. *Consider the information needs of minority groups:* Information materials should be available to cater for a variety of users, including those from minority ethnic groups, non-English speakers, people with disabilities, and so on. Some patients may prefer to receive only basic information while others will want more detail, so there is likely to be a need for a range of materials on a particular topic. Evidence from this study suggested that information producers were more likely to under-estimate the amount of detail required than to over-estimate it, but introductory materials have a place as long as they provide details of where to find further information for those who want it.

5. Review the clinical research evidence and use systematic reviews wherever possible: It is very important that patient information is based on the best and most up-to-date information available. Our study demonstrated that in many cases patients were being provided with inaccurate, misleading or biased information. Reliance on the knowledge of individual clinicians is not sufficient as a guarantee of reliability. Descriptive information on the causes of the condition, its prevalence and natural history can be drawn from epidemiological studies, which should be carefully reviewed. The most reliable way to ensure that information on treatment efficacy is scientifically-based and accurate is to conduct a systematic review of the research literature, or to base it on a review contained in a quality-assured database such as the Cochrane Library (Update Software 1998). This information will require adaptation to make it suitable for patients, but it should reduce the chance of inaccuracies.

6. Plan how the materials can be used within a wider programme promoting shared decision-making: Information for patients is a necessary component of shared decision-making, but it will be insufficient if clinicians are not prepared to encourage patient participation. Health professionals require training in how to meet patients' information needs and how to elicit their preferences and incorporate them into clinical decision-making. Developers of patient information materials should consider how they are to be used in clinical practice and provide support for clinicians who are prepared to distribute the materials.

7. Consider cost and feasibility of distribution and updating when choosing media: There are many important practical considerations when deciding on which media to use. Leaflets can be relatively cheap to produce and disseminate, but they are less appropriate for people with reading difficulties. Once in circulation it is difficult to control their use and people may get hold of out-of-date versions. Audio-tapes avoid the problem of reading ability, but some people find it difficult to remember information heard on a tape. Telephone helplines can be made widely and cheaply accessible, but the quality of telephone lines can be variable so they should be regularly tested for audibility. Video has the advantage of providing both sound and pictures and offers the possibility of including interviews with patients describing their experiences, but it is more expensive to produce and can be difficult to update. Computer-based factsheets are cheap to produce, but current examples tend to be visually boring. Interactive media, such as CD-Rom with a touch-screen facility, offer the possibility of tailoring information to an individual patient's particular needs or preferences, but require access to a computer. Web sites can be easily updated, but many people do not have access to the Internet. There is no ideal solution, but it is important to consider the target audience and how they will access the information before opting for a particular platform. Combinations of media can be very effective, for example videos with accompanying leaflets, or CD-Rom with links to a Web site for updating.

8. *Develop a strategy for distribution*: Some materials are designed to be 'prescribed' by clinicians during consultations, others are intended for wide distribution to anyone interested. Method of distribution needs to be carefully thought through and planned accordingly. The need to ensure that patients have access to up-to-date information may argue for targeted distribution via clinicians. On the other hand, many patients find it difficult to get hold of information from their doctors and seek help instead from consumer health information services, public libraries, pharmacies, etc. A statement of the intended uses should be included together with an indication of the most appropriate timing of the information in relation to the care pathway.

9. *Evaluate the materials and their use*: Patients and professionals should be involved in evaluating the materials during development and afterwards, to ensure they are achieving their stated goals.

10. *Make arrangements for periodic review and updating*: It is very important that information materials are reviewed regularly to see if they need to be updated.

11. *Publicise the availability of the information materials*: Since patients find it so hard to get hold of good information, it is important that good materials receive wide publicity so that people – both patients and clinicians – know of their existence. The existence of information providers, for example consumer health information services, also needs to be better publicised.

The content

1. *Use patients' questions as the starting point*: Decisions about content should start from the questions patients want answers to. As our study has shown, patients want to understand the causes of the problem and the treatment options. They want to know about things they can do to help

Box 5 Common questions asked by patients

- What is causing the problem?
- Am I alone? How does my experience compare with that of other patients?
- Is there anything I can do myself to ameliorate the problem or prevent recurrence?
- What is the purpose of the tests and investigations?
- What are the different treatment options?
- What are the benefits of the treatment(s)?
- What are the risks of the treatment(s)?
- How likely are the benefits and risks?
- Is it essential to have treatment for this problem?
- Will the treatment(s) relieve the symptoms?
- How long will it take to recover?
- What are the possible side-effects?
- What effect will the treatment(s) have on my feelings and emotions?
- What effect will the treatment(s) have on my sex life?
- How will it affect my risk of disease in the future?
- How can I prepare myself for the treatment?
- What procedures will be followed if I go to hospital?
- When can I go home?
- What do my carers need to know?
- What can I do to speed recovery?
- What are the options for rehabilitation?
- Where can I get hold of more information about the problem or treatments?

themselves and they want balanced information about risks as well as benefits. Information about complementary therapies is also wanted, together with an honest assessment of likely efficacy. As a rough guide to content, Box 5 outlines a set of questions commonly asked by patients.

2.   Ensure that common concerns and misconceptions are addressed: Some research may be necessary at an early stage in the development of the materials to discover patients' specific concerns and beliefs. It is important to allay any unnecessary fears based on misconceptions about the health problem or its treatment. If patients' perceptions are in contradiction to the evidence from reliable research, it is particularly important to explain the basis for the discrepancies.

3.   Refer to all relevant treatment or management options: It is important to include information about all relevant options, not just those which are most common or those for which there is good evidence on efficacy. Patients may have heard about a variety of possible treatments and will find information about these useful, even if they are not recommended.

4. Include honest information about benefits and risks: Information should be balanced and include a careful and honest assessment of the pros and cons of treatment derived from good quality research and systematic reviews. It is important to avoid over-emphasis on benefits (leading to a misleadingly optimistic view of treatment efficacy) or risks (leading to an unduly pessimistic view). If outcome probabilities are unknown because relevant research has not been carried out, it is best to be frank about this rather than provide reassurance which may turn out to be false.

5. Include quantitative information where possible: It is not always easy to explain outcome probabilities and risk, but simple techniques can be helpful such as use of diagrams to explain percentages. Patients need to be able to understand potential risks and benefits in a context which is meaningful for them. It is important to pay careful attention to possible biases caused by the way in which the information is 'framed'. As a general rule, one should be aiming for a balanced but non-alarmist approach.

6. Include checklists and questions to ask the doctor: Patients appreciate features in leaflets which actively engage them and help them to record relevant information for discussion in a clinical consultation such as symptom diaries or space to write down questions or points to remember.

7. Include sources of further information: Lists of further reading and details of relevant consumer or self-help groups are greatly appreciated.

8. Use non-alarmist, non-patronising language in active rather than passive voice: Patients prefer information which is reassuring and non-alarmist, honest, down-to-earth and practical, and which relates to them personally. It should be clear and easy to read, technical words should be explained, and the material should be tested for readability. The language should be facilitative rather than prescriptive, promoting a participative approach and avoiding a 'doctor knows best' attitude which many patients find patronising. Use of active rather than passive voice is preferable. It is important to avoid victim-blaming or dismissing patients' concerns.

9. Design should be structured and concise with good illustrations: The material should be structured and concise, with clear headings, important sections highlighted, short blocks of text and well indexed. The design and layout should look professional. Print should be large and uncluttered. Illustrations are very helpful for illuminating particular points in the text, but 'gory' pictures are not appreciated.

10. Be explicit about authorship and sponsorship: Some of the materials reviewed provided no information about who had written them, making it difficult to check reliability. The names of authors, advisers and sponsors should always be included in patient information materials.

11. Include reference to sources and strength of evidence: It is very helpful for those wanting to assess the reliability of the information if the material includes explicit reference to the sources from which it was drawn. Patients need information about the strength of evidence on which the information is based.

12. Include the publication date: If a publication date is not included, it is very difficult to judge whether or not the information is likely to be up to date.

A role for the NHS Executive and health authorities

This study has demonstrated the potential value of good quality patient information materials and serious deficiencies among many materials currently in use in the NHS. The goals of the *Patient's Charter* and the Patient Partnership strategy will not be met unless patients are provided with good quality information about diseases and treatments. There are strong grounds for believing that investment in the development of patient information materials will prove cost-effective. This proposition needs further evaluation, but in the meantime it is clear that patients' information needs are not being met.

We urge the NHS Executive to take the following steps:

- Fund the development and evaluation of high quality patient information materials covering common clinical problems.
- Commission patient information materials to accompany the evidence-based clinical guidelines to be developed by the National Institute of Clinical Excellence.
- Establish a system for accrediting patient information materials and Web sites to help patients and health professionals identify reliable information.

Health authorities could support the process by:

- Establishing a system for disseminating good quality materials to patients. Where appropriate this might include making them available in GP surgeries, hospital departments, community pharmacies, consumer health information services, healthy living centres, public libraries, etc.

- Ensuring that each NHS trust and primary care group has a designated senior member of staff responsible for ensuring that patient information materials meet high quality standards.
- Ensuring that all clinicians receive training in communication skills and techniques to promote shared decision-making.

Part 2

Reviews of the materials

This part includes details of the focus group participants and the academic specialists and their reactions to each of the individual materials, organised into chapters according to the health topics.

Each chapter begins with a summary of the patients' and specialists' views, followed by reviews of the individual materials. Rankings and summary scores given by patients and specialists are provided for each leaflet, tape or video, together with the specialists' ratings of specific characteristics, i.e. a score out of 5 for comprehensibility and readability, style and tone, explaining technical terms, visual appeal, general information about the condition, information about causes of the problem, information about likely consequences, self-help, including lifestyle changes and coping strategies, coverage of uncertainties or gaps in the scientific knowledge, whether it gives a balanced view of the treatment options, and whether it provides sufficient information to make informed choices.

Chapter 10

Back pain

Focus group

The focus group comprised six women aged between 17 and over 60, and two men aged 43 and over 50. All had had back problems for at least two years, and several had severe, chronic problems stemming from congenital defects or accidents. All had tried several treatments and the group's test and treatment repertoire was broad, including various drug regimes, massage, hot and cold packs, attendance at specialised pain clinics, yoga, Alexander technique, chiropractic, osteopathy, physiotherapy and surgery.

The group members were generally pragmatic and long-suffering. Their stories all involved tales of positive and negative encounters with health care professionals, and a certain amount of trial and error in attempts to treat and cope with their back problems. They emphasised a need to manage the frustration and psychological consequences of back pain and to 'work out what works for you'.

The group recognised that they were not the typical sufferers of acute low back pain for whom the leaflets were primarily intended.

Academic specialists

The specialist reviewers included a professor of general practice, a senior lecturer in general practice, and a senior lecturer in rehabilitation, all of whom had a particular interest in back pain.

The materials

Don't Let Back Pain Spoil Your Life: East Lancashire Health Authority
Understanding Acute Low Back Problems: Agency for Health Care Policy and Research (AHCPR US Dept of Health and Human Services)
Nurofen Guide: Crookes Healthcare in association with the National Back Pain Association
The Back Book: The Stationery Office
Back Strain/Pain: PatientWise, Wiley and Sons Ltd

Rankings

	Patients	Specialists
1	AHCPR	The Stationery Office
2	Crookes Healthcare	AHCPR
3	The Stationery Office	East Lancs HA
4	PatientWise	Crookes Healthcare
5	East Lancs HA	PatientWise

Summary of reviews

Only printed materials on back pain were assessed, including three booklets, one leaflet and a factsheet. Patients and specialists differed in their rankings of these materials. The patients were particularly enthusiastic about the booklet produced by the US Agency for Health Care Policy and Research (AHCPR), which was also highly commended by the specialists. The specialists gave even higher ratings to *The Back Book*, which was produced by a group of academic researchers (including two of the specialist reviewers) and published by the Stationery Office. While some patients were enthusiastic about this booklet, others were quite critical, disliking its tone and presentational style. The *Nurofen Guide* published by Crookes Healthcare was well received by the patients but the specialists disliked it, giving it low ratings for accuracy, completeness and balance. Both groups were lukewarm about the leaflet produced by East Lancashire Health Authority which provided introductory information fairly well, but was felt to be too lacking in detail to be really useful. The specialists were highly critical of the PatientWise factsheet which was seen as out of date and inaccurate. Only two out of the five materials reviewed – the AHCPR booklet and *The Back Book* – were considered by specialists to be helpful in promoting informed decision-making. The other materials were criticised for containing inaccurate or misleading information and omissions.

Don't Let Back Pain Spoil Your Life: East Lancashire Health Authority

Overall ratings:	Patients	4.4 (range 1–7) rank 5 (out of 5)
	Specialists	5.7 (range 2–8) rank 3

Publication date: March 1997 (no date on leaflet)

Address: East Lancashire Health Authority, 31–33 Kenyon Road, Lomeshaye Estate, Nelson, Lancs BB9 5SZ.

Description

Consisting of one A4 sheet folded into three, this leaflet has a black and white photo of a bicycle chain on the front and a cartoon inside. The message on the cover says 'Keep moving'. It includes sections on: back pain – the facts; what you can do to help yourself; what your doctor can do; other sources of support. There are three accompanying posters, one with the bicycle chain photo in colour, one entitled 'Back pain – the facts', and another 'Back pain – what you can do'. Developed by members of a health education department as part of a project to implement clinical guidelines for the management of acute back pain, the leaflet aims to encourage self management of simple back pain. It is intended for use by anyone who suffers from back pain. Information was drawn from the report of the Clinical Standards Advisory Group and other health education literature. It was piloted with patients and professionals during development.

Patients' views

People in the focus group expressed divergent views about this leaflet. While some thought it might be a useful introductory leaflet for people who had just started to have back pain, others disputed its usefulness in any situation. Features which were commented on favourably included the suggestions about what people with back pain can do to help themselves (although members of the focus group identified several practical things which they felt should also have been included), the inclusion of contact addresses and the simplicity of the language. On the negative side, people mentioned that it was 'very, very simple but not very informative' and 'superficial'. There was general agreement that it did not give a fair reflection of available treatment options, and some concern that although the leaflet provided addresses of national associations for osteopathy, chiropractic and physiotherapy, it did not adequately explain what these treatments were or what the associations did. Several people felt that the leaflet was 'dismissive in tone'.

Academic specialists' views

The leaflet was commended by the specialist reviewers for appropriately discouraging bedrest and encouraging activity. It mentioned use of cold pack and heat, but omitted many commonly used treatments such as physiotherapy, manipulation, surgery, TENS, traction, acupuncture, ultrasound and specific exercises. There was felt to be insufficient information on outcome probabilities and on risks.

The specialists gave this leaflet high scores for readability, style, visual appeal and for general information about the clinical condition. It was seen as providing 'simple, fairly accurate information' but with 'not a lot of detail'. One reviewer did not like the picture on the front cover, remarking that the analogy of a bicycle chain and spine was inappropriate and confusing because it implied that the spine could get jammed or broken. The illustration misleadingly suggested that the spine ought to be straight.

The leaflet scored low on coverage of uncertainties and knowledge gaps and on the whole, experts did not feel it presented a balanced view because it failed to mention treatment options offered by physiotherapists, osteopaths and chiropractors. Since it included no technical terms, specialists did not give it a rating for this characteristic. None of the subject specialists felt it gave patients the information they would need to make an informed choice about treatment.

Don't let back pain spoil your life: East Lancashire Health Authority

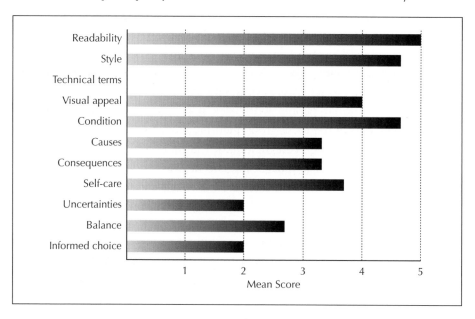

Understanding Acute Low Back Problems: Agency for Health Care Policy and Research, US Dept of Health and Human Services

Overall ratings: Patients   8.3 (range 6–9) rank 1
                       Specialists   7.7 (range 6–9) rank 2

Publication date: December 1994

Address: Agency for Health Care Policy and Research, Publications Clearinghouse, PO Box 8547, Silver Spring, MD 20907, USA.

Description

This 14-page booklet was produced in the USA by the Agency for Health Care Policy and Research (AHCPR). The information it contains is based on the AHCPR clinical guideline on acute low back problems in adults, which was developed by a panel of experts. It includes two anatomical diagrams and a drawing showing safe lifting and carrying positions. It contains the following sections: purpose of leaflet; about the back; causes of low back problems; things to do about low back problems; getting relief; physical activity; bed rest; about work and family; things you can do now; exercise; if you are not getting better; about surgery; prevention of low back problems; when low back symptoms return; while your back is getting better; for further information; space to record medical history; questions to ask your health care provider.

Patients' views

This leaflet was highly rated quite consistently by the people in the focus group. It was generally perceived as 'well thought out' and likely to be useful. It was suggested that the leaflet would give people a basic understanding of what was wrong, and encourage them to get involved by starting to look at their problem and thinking about what to ask doctors. However, the lack of information about chiropractic and osteopathy was noted.

Features particularly liked included: the section which asked questions encouraging people to think about their condition and preparing them to answer questions from health professionals and to ask questions of them; the clear purpose and structure of the leaflet, including the highlighted sections; and the upbeat, positive tone and jargon-free language.

The group realised that the leaflet was not produced in the UK, but most felt that the substitution of UK addresses for the back page would make it suitable for use here.

Academic specialists' views

All the main treatment options were covered in this booklet. All ratings by the specialists were positive, i.e. 3 or above. The booklet scored high on description of the clinical condition, and on readability and style, with specialists commending it for its comprehensiveness and for providing an accurate reflection of current evidence. However, one reviewer commented that there was insufficient emphasis on self-help, encouraging dependency on a health provider.

It contained comprehensive information about treatments and scored high for balance, although reviewers felt it stressed benefits more than risks and gave insufficient information about outcome probabilities. The specialists gave it a high rating for facilitating informed choices, although they felt that prevention was slightly underplayed and surgery over-emphasised.

Understanding acute low back problems: AHCPR

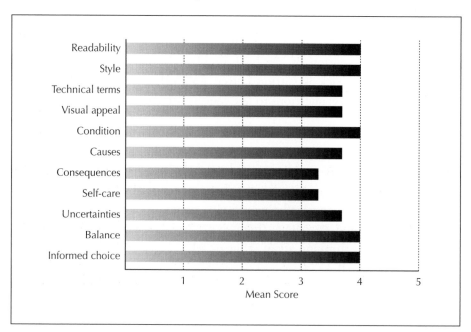

Nurofen Guide: Crookes Healthcare in association with The National Back Pain Association

Overall ratings: Patients   7.1 (range 3–10) rank 2

                        Specialists   2.3 (range 1–3) rank 4

Publication date: No date on booklet.

Address: The Nurofen Advisory Service, PO Box 193,

                        Nottingham NG3 2HA.

Description

This is a 16-page booklet copiously illustrated with colour photographs, including five photographs of Nurofen packs. It includes sections on: backs in focus; back to basics; what makes your back ache? tips for a trouble-free back; easing the pain; professional help; guidelines for the safe use of painkillers; know your Nurofen.

Patients' views

This leaflet was, with a few exceptions, quite highly rated by focus group participants. The fact that it was produced by the makers of Nurofen as well as the National Back Pain Association had been quickly noticed, and several people said that the obvious advertising would have deterred them from picking up the leaflet in, for example, a GP's surgery or a pharmacy shop. Having read it, however, the majority view was that, leaving the advertising aside, most of the information and advice contained in the leaflet was useful. They appreciated the fact that it covered a range of treatment and self-help options, including osteopathy, chiropractic, physiotherapy, and Alexander technique.

Comments about the organisation of the material and the language used were mainly positive. Opinions were divided about the appropriateness and acceptability of the illustrations: some felt the people portrayed were too young and glamorous. There was general agreement that the leaflet could be useful for people with new acute back problems.

Subject specialists' views

Very little information about treatment efficacy was included in this booklet. Specialists noted that simple painkillers such as paracetamol and aspirin were not mentioned and information about TENS, traction, biofeedback, heat and cold treatment was omitted. There was virtually no information about prognosis or risks. The specialists felt that this booklet was primarily an advertising vehicle for Nurofen.

Although it scored high for style and visual appeal, it received low ratings for its description of the clinical condition and possible causes and for information about benefits and risks. Specialists considered the information misleading and alarmist in places. One said: 'A lot of money has obviously gone into this glossy booklet, but it is a pure advertising vehicle for Nurofen. Although the illustrations and layout are eye catching, the message is seriously biased.'

Nurofen guide: Crookes Healthcare

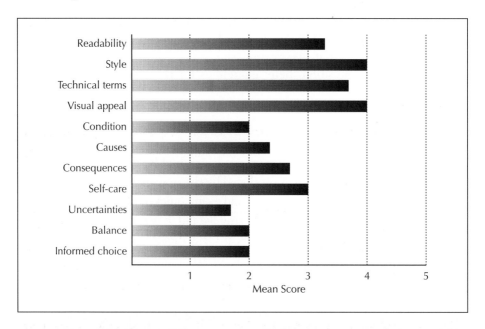

The Back Book: The Stationery Office

Overall ratings:	Patients	6.9 (range 0–10) rank 3
	Specialists	8.0 (range 7–9) rank 1

Publication date: No date on booklet.

Address: The Stationery Office Ltd, St Crispins, Duke Street, Norwich NR3 1PD.

Description

Written by a multi-disciplinary group of researchers from general practice, orthopaedics, physiotherapy, osteopathy, psychology, and rehabilitation (including two of the specialist reviewers), the 23 page booklet was designed for patients with acute back pain for use mainly in the primary care setting. Sections include: back facts; causes of back pain; rest or active exercise; exercise is good for you; staying active; how to stay active; when to see your doctor; it's your back. It is illustrated with simple line drawings and includes a section for users to note down things that help them and things that make their pain worse.

It aims to encourage patients with back pain to resume their normal activities as soon as possible and to promote self-help. The content is based on the RCGP guidelines on the management of back pain. Patients were not directly involved in the production of the booklet, but the developers report that it has been evaluated and found to be accessible and acceptable. It is currently being used in two randomised controlled trials.

Patients' views

This booklet split opinions within the focus group, whose ratings of it ranged to both extremes of the scale. Some of the disagreement revolved around the style and tone of the leaflet. Several of those who disliked the leaflet described it as 'patronising' and 'victim blaming'. A woman who had been suffering from severe chronic back pain for some time felt the leaflet judged her negatively and implied (with statements like 'back pain need not cripple you unless you let it') that her inability to do certain things was her own fault. On the other hand, some people liked the 'positive attitude' of the leaflet, the fact that it gave the patient some responsibility and made them feel in control.

Personal experiences led several members of the group to dispute the accuracy of the information provided, and the availability of some of the recommended treatments (such as early initiation of physiotherapy) in an NHS context. Information about different treatment options was generally felt to be limited, but a minority of people thought the booklet would be a useful introduction for new back pain sufferers. The general presentation of the leaflet was thought to be poor.

Subject specialists' views

The information about treatment options was considered fairly comprehensive although it lacked information about popular treatments which are unsupported by evidence of efficacy, such as TENS, traction, massage, biofeedback, acupuncture, ultrasound, injections and back corsets. There was little information about outcome probabilities.

In general the specialists liked this booklet. It achieved high scores for most aspects but was judged relatively poor at communicating uncertainties. The specialist reviewers felt it provided an accurate reflection of the evidence-base. The messages were considered to be simple, clear and positive; and it was seen as defusing the problem and appropriately encouraging self-help and coping. The style was commended for its simplicity and accessibility. The illustrations were criticised for occasionally not matching the text and it was felt that the cover could have been more eye-catching.

One of the specialist reviewers was principal author of the booklet, and another was a contributor, so they cannot be said to be unbiased. The one reviewer not involved in its production described the booklet positively: 'comprehensive and reflects current evidence well', although he felt the tone was patronising in places.

The Back Book: The Stationery Office

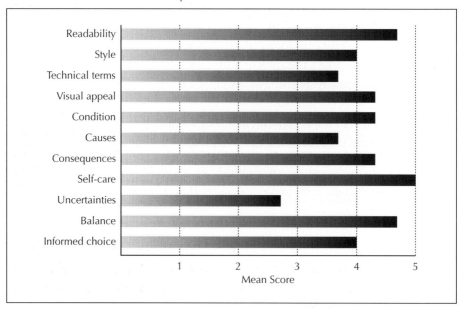

Back Strain/Pain: PatientWise, pub. Wiley

Overall ratings: Patients   5.6 (range 1–9) rank 4
     Specialists   1.7 (range 1–3) rank 5

Publication date: 1995

Address: PatientWise, John Wiley & Sons Ltd, 1 Oldlands Way, Bognor Regis, West Sussex, PO22 9SA.

Description

This factsheet is part of a patient information system that comes in two formats: a loose-leaf volume for photocopying and a software version from which individual sheets can be printed out for patients' use. It includes a paragraph on each of the following: what is it?; how does it occur?; why does it occur?; what does treatment/management involve?; what to watch out for during treatment; what to watch out for after treatment; what would happen if the condition was not treated?; what is involved for family and friends?

Developed by a physician, a GP and a lay editor, the factsheet has been tested by patients and assessed for readability using the Gunning Fog Index. A formal evaluation of the PatientWise system was published in the *Journal of the Royal Society of Medicine* 1996; 89: 557–60.

Patients' views

Most of the focus group members rated this sheet relatively low because they found it 'too technical', 'too long and boring', and 'depressing'. One person had looked at it, but thought that if she was feeling ill she would have found it really off-putting, and admitted she hadn't bothered to read it. Another dismissed it as 'pseudo science'. Several people felt it more suitable for health professionals than for patients, and one man commented that people would need to be informed before they read it.

The people who rated the leaflet highest liked the fact that the sheet mentioned some rare conditions, that it included 'good background information' and 'scientific information'. The section about 'family and friends' was commented on positively.

Academic specialists' views

Specialists were critical of the fact that, contrary to the latest evidence, the factsheet recommended bedrest for back pain. The factsheet received low ratings for its description of the condition and its causes, for information about self-care, uncertainties, balance, technical terms, visual appeal and promoting informed choice. Average scores were achieved for coverage of the consequences of back pain and for style and readability. Specialists thought it boring and lacking visual appeal. It provided no information about popular treatments such as TENS, traction, biofeedback, ultrasound, manipulation and no information about the risks of any treatment or about uncertainties or knowledge gaps.

The factsheet was criticised by one reviewer for giving inaccurate advice and for promoting an old-fashioned medical model: 'Too much emphasis on being careful – encourages a passive, dependent attitude. Encourages rest rather than activity.'

Back strain/pain: PatientWise, pub. Wiley and Sons Ltd

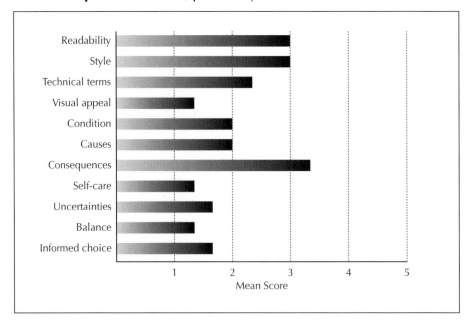

Chapter 11

Cataract

Focus group

Three women and two men in their 50s and 60s participated in this focus group. Three of the participants had retired from paid employment (one from a secretarial position and two from 'professional' positions). One continued to work as a secretary and one in computing.

All five participants reported slow deterioration of their eyesight over several years, and all had undergone successful cataract operations within the previous two years. One person had had two operations, and another two were facing second operations in the future. One participant reported having pushed for early treatment, while another felt she had 'left it late'.

Academic specialists

Reviewers included a consultant in public health medicine and a non-medical epidemiologist, both of whom had carried out research into patients' experiences of cataract surgery, and a specialist in ophthalmic epidemiology.

The materials

Cataracts and Their Treatment: Gloucester Day Case Cataract Unit
Cataract: Buckinghamshire Health Authority with NHS Centre for Reviews and Dissemination
Understanding Cataracts: Royal National Institute for the Blind
Cataract Surgery: Wallsgrave Hospitals NHS Trust
Cataracts: United Bristol Healthcare NHS Trust

Rankings

	Patients	*Specialists*
1	Gloucester	Buckinghamshire
2	Bristol	Bristol
3	Buckinghamshire	Gloucester
4	RNIB	RNIB (3=)
5	Wallsgrave	Wallsgrave

Summary of reviews

Materials reviewed included an audiotape and accompanying booklet (Gloucester Day Case Unit), a video with supporting literature (Bristol NHS Trust), and three booklets. The only disagreement between patients' and specialists' rankings was about the relative merits of the Gloucester audiotape and the Buckinghamshire booklet. The patients liked the way the tape presented information for people who were going to have surgery, although it did not cover alternatives. The specialists commended the Buckinghamshire booklet for being explicitly evidence-based and for promoting shared decision-making. None of the other materials was considered comprehensive enough to be helpful to patients wanting to participate in decisions about their care.

Cataracts and Their Treatment: Gloucester Day Case Cataract Unit, sponsored by Pharmacia Ophthalmics

---

Overall ratings: Patients   8.4 (range 6–10) rank 1 (out of 5)

                            Specialists   4.7 (range 4–6) rank 3=

Publication date: 1994

Address: Gloucestershire Royal Hospital, Great Western Road, Gloucester, GL1 3NN.

Description

An audiotape and accompanying booklet designed primarily to provide information about what patients can expect when they come into hospital for surgery and afterwards in post-operative care. It also includes information about the condition and options for treatment. The main sections are: what is a cataract? pre-operative care; the cataract operation; post-operative care and recovery.

The tape is designed especially for patients who cannot read even relatively large print and is distributed at the pre-admission clinic, three weeks prior to surgery. The booklet and tape script were written by a multidisciplinary team following consultation with patients about their information needs. The materials have been evaluated and the developers hope to produce versions in Hindi and Urdu.

Patients' views

The participants recognised that the tape was for people who were going to have surgery, so it did not cover other options and was not meant to support decisions. They thought there should be an 'earlier' tape to help people decide whether to have an operation, and if so what type of operation and anaesthetic to have. There was not enough information about the risks of the surgery but some people said again that they would prefer to have been told about these at an earlier stage. The procedural information was interesting and given clearly. One of the participants who had already had surgery said that she would not have been so worried during and after her operation if she had been given this information beforehand. Several people observed that it didn't provide the information about post-operative follow up and self-care which they felt would have been useful.

The participants all liked the voice of the narrator and appreciated the reassuring but non-condescending way in which information was presented.

Academic specialists' views

This tape assumes that the decision to undergo surgery has been taken, so it does not discuss alternatives such as watchful waiting. No information is provided on the benefits and risks of different options.

The specialists considered the tape easy to listen to, using clear and comprehensible language, but the tone was patronising and somewhat autocratic which led one reviewer to comment: 'The three 'do nots' were: (1) no rubbing, (2) no bending below the waist (how do you put your pants/knickers on?), (3) no exertion', for all of which the subject specialist thought there was a lack of evidence.

It provided helpful details on what happens during the hospital stay, but did not promote informed choice. The specialists recognised that it was probably not designed for this purpose: 'If it is to tell people what to expect while receiving treatment, then it does a good job, though the information on post-operative care is not evidence-based. If the tape is the only information received by a person who may need a cataract operation, then many extra points and issues need to be covered.'

Cataracts and their treatment: Gloucester Day Case Cataract Unit

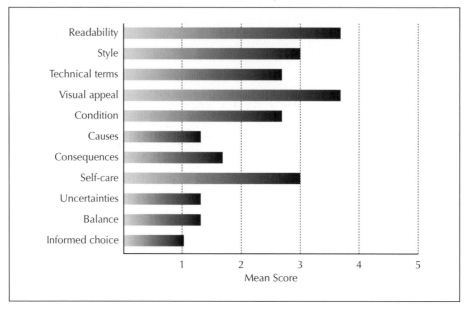

Mean Score

Cataract: Buckinghamshire Health Authority and the Cataract
Focus Group in collaboration with the NHS Centre for Reviews
and Dissemination, University of York

Overall ratings: Patients   7.7 (range 5–10) rank 3
                      Specialists   6.7 (range 6–7) rank 1

Publication date: 1996

Address: Buckinghamshire Health Authority, 1–7 The Courtyard,
                      Merlin Centre, Gatehouse Close, Aylesbury, Bucks
                      HP19 3DP.

Description

This leaflet was designed to inform patients about cataract and to give them
information about the treatment options. It is intended to be prescribed to
patients by optometrists and GPs. Designed for older people with age-related
cataract, it is a 12-page A5 leaflet printed on stiff yellow paper using large sans
serif font. It has one illustration showing a cross section view of the eye.
Contents include: what is cataract?; how do I know if I have cataract?; why do

people get cataract?; what can I do?; should I have an operation?; types of operation; anaesthetic – local or general?; day case or overnight?; what are the results of the operation?; myths you may have heard about cataract; questions for your consultant; personal patient information; my questions.

Patient focus groups informed the content and the layout of the leaflet, together with research evidence from a systematic review of the literature. A version for professionals was also produced and patients can request this version if they wish to. The same process was used to develop the professional leaflet, drawing on the views of GPs, optometrists, nurses, anaesthetists, ophthalmologists and patients' representatives. The leaflet has been formally and informally evaluated by the developers.

Patients' views

Most members of the focus group rated this leaflet quite highly, but one person felt it was 'too general' and 'not particularly useful to her'. There was agreement that the leaflet would be helpful for people facing decisions about whether or not to have an operation (the checklist of symptoms/problems experienced was favourably commented on), and one woman noted that 'a lot of the questions were the sort of questions that do concern people'. People who had had difficulties communicating with consultants, however, were amused at the suggestions in the leaflet of issues that should be discussed with doctors.

Opinions differed about the value of mentioning in the leaflet that surgeons varied in the amount of experience they have, and that not all surgeons could do particular types of operation. The leaflet was felt to lack detail about the different types of operation, and about operative procedures.

The contents page and layout were generally liked, and the fact that the producers had known to print the leaflet on yellow paper suggested that they understood the problem and had taken care when producing the leaflet.

Academic specialists' views

Two of the academic specialists were involved in the production of this leaflet, which was explicitly evidence-based and in the view of the specialists promoted shared decision-making. The leaflet was thought to include good coverage of the risks and benefits of the treatment options, including assessment procedures, medical and surgical treatments and watchful waiting.

One specialist noted that no information was provided on different types of surgery, or on the risks and benefits of anaesthesia or laser treatment. The choice of matt yellow paper and sans serif font were commended: 'all good for the visually impaired (backed by evidence)'.

On the whole this leaflet was considered successful in its aim of promoting informed choice based on clear unbiased information. One reviewer commented that the leaflet was helpful in making choices about whether or not to have surgery, but it provided little detail on the various types of surgical procedures.

Cataract: Buckinghamshire Health Authority

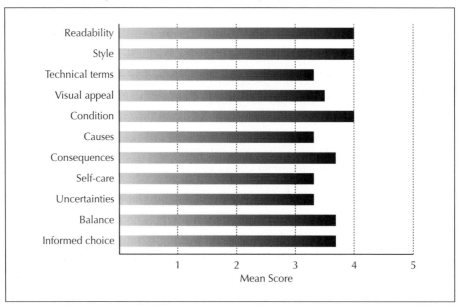

Understanding Cataracts: Royal National Institute for the Blind/
Royal College of Ophthalmologists

Overall ratings:	Patients	6.8 (range 2–9) rank 4 (out of 5)
	Specialists	4.7 (range 4–6) rank 3=
Publication date:	1996	
Address:	Royal National Institute for the Blind, 224 Great Portland Street, London W1N 6AA.	

Description

This 12-page booklet in large print, black on white, includes one diagram of the eye. It contains sections on: what is a cataract?; the lens; what causes a cataract?; some symptoms; seeing double; poor vision in bright light; change of colour vision; what can be done to help?; what is a lens implant?; when should I have the operation?; what happens in the operation?; after the operation; about the Royal National Institute for the Blind; about the Royal College of Ophthalmologists; further information.

Patients' views

Participants varied greatly in their ratings of this leaflet. Those who rated it low had found it uninformative, criticising it particularly for not mentioning that there are different types of operations, different types of anaesthetic and different implant strengths. Those rating it highly had focused more on its positive and friendly tone. The description of symptoms was also favourably commented on by several people, and the list of contact addresses was thought to be useful.

Several people were particularly disappointed with the leaflet because they would have expected the consumer organisation which produced it to come up with something more informative.

Academic specialists' views

Specialists pointed out that this leaflet covers surgical and medical treatments, but implies that watchful waiting is not a serious option. It was criticised for failing to discuss alternative surgical treatments and for providing little information on outcome probabilities or risks of the various options. Assessment of vision was not discussed in any detail. One specialist reviewer commented: 'It explains the symptoms and that the decision to operate should depend on 'interference with your ability to read, to work, or to do the things you enjoy', but it does not mention the general concept of quality of life and uses the term 'visual impairment' without explaining this.' Information about post-operative care was limited and specialists criticised it for failing to give a realistic assessment of risk and how to cope with anxiety about the operation.

The style and presentation of the leaflet was commended: 'Large print – sans serif font used. Not glossy – good for glare – but would be better in yellow (evidence supports this).' The language was considered to be friendly and reasonably empowering, but in general it was not felt to be particularly helpful in promoting informed choice.

Understanding cataracts: Royal National Institute for the Blind

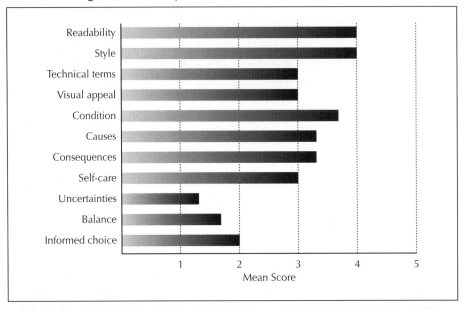

Overall ratings:	Patients	5.2 (range 1–10) rank 5
	Specialists	2.7 (range 1–5) rank 5

Publication date: No date on leaflet.

Address: Wallsgrave Hospitals NHS Trust, Clifford Bridge Road, Wallsgrave, Coventry CV2 2DX.

Description

A black print leaflet on white paper with large sans serif print, with ten pages and four drawings, it includes sections on: your questions answered after cataract surgery; what is a cataract?; when will I be discharged from hospital?; can I do the cooking?; will I be safe at home alone?; can I do the housework?; can I have a bath?; fresh air and exercise; when can I return to work?; do I need to rest?; when can I drive?; will I need to attend the hospital after discharge?;

will my glasses need changing?; will I need eye drops after discharge?; the following instructions should help you; how to use your eye drops and ointment; storage of eye drops and ointment.

Patients' views

Again participants' ratings of this leaflet varied greatly. To some extent the variation appeared to reflect the extent to which people agreed with the advice that was given about post-operative activity. The leaflet suggested that things would be very difficult for quite a few weeks after the operation, and placed a lot of restrictions on activity during that period. It was felt by some to be negative in tone.

On the positive side, the explanation (including diagrams) of how to use eyedrops was thought to be helpful and the large print of the leaflet was appreciated.

Subject specialists' views

The specialists pointed out that this leaflet assumes that the decision to undergo surgery has been taken, so alternative treatments and watchful waiting are not covered. It was criticised for containing no information about prevalence and very little on symptoms and for saying nothing about the benefits and risks of surgery or alternative surgical treatments, such as phakoemulsification. Specialists felt the style was autocratic and the content inaccurate: 'Old fashioned, outdated, wrong information, not evidence based. Alarming. Dictatorial. Offensive. Bossy!' They considered that its prescriptive and patronising style did nothing to promote shared decision-making.

Cataract surgery: Wallsgrave Hospitals NHS Trust

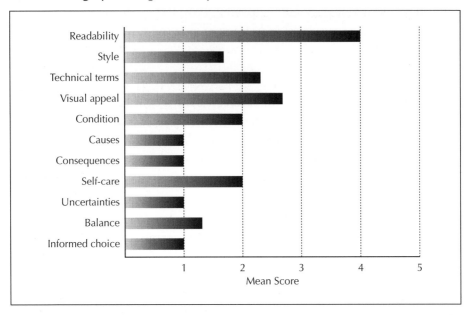

Cataracts: A clearer vision for the future: The United Bristol
Healthcare NHS Trust

Overall ratings: Patients   8.0 (range 6–10) rank 2
                     Specialists 6.0 (range 5–7) rank 2

Publication date: 1996

Address: United Bristol Healthcare NHS Trust, Marlborough
                     Street, Bristol, Avon BS1 3NU.

Description

This video with supporting literature contains information on: the effects of
cataracts; the assessment of patients; the treatment of cataracts; post-operative
care; application of eye medication; application of an eye shield. The professionally
made video was intended to provide background information about the
condition, treatments and post-operative care. Designed for use mainly by
elderly patients and carers, the video is also provided to promote the hospital
to purchasers and GPs. Five leaflets are used to supplement the material in the

video. These cover: about your cataract; local anaesthetic; general anaesthetic; post operative instructions; how to use your eye drops.

The content was developed in consultation with medical staff, nurses and patients, and comments were sought from district nurses and GPs. It has been evaluated by questionnaire and by seeking verbal comments.

Patients' views

The video was given quite high ratings by all participants. There was quite a lot of discussion about its potential value for families. The visuals which compared normal sight with cataract impaired sight were judged to be useful in conveying to family members some of the problems that people with cataracts might be having, and the portrayal in the video of the family as being involved in the treatment was liked.

The lack of detail about different treatment options was commented on (only one type of operation was shown), but the video was generally thought to be reassuring viewing for people who were going to have surgery.

Academic specialists' views

The specialist reviewers liked much about this video, in particular the information about the condition and the symptoms and the information on post-operative care. Language and images were felt to be clear and the presentation was seen as positive and empowering. However, only one treatment option, day case phakoemulsification, was presented in any detail. One reviewer commented that this was probably the best treatment option according to current evidence, but they felt that it did not promote shared decision-making since it failed to provide information about the alternatives.

Some treatment options, for example other methods of removing the cataract surgically, alternatives to implants, and watchful waiting were not covered in the video, which the specialists felt provided little information about risks and outcome probabilities.

Cataracts: United Bristol Healthcare NHS Trust

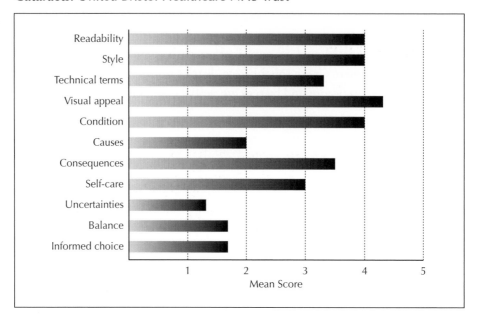

Chapter 12

Depression

Focus group

This focus group comprised six women and two men whose ages ranged from 33 to 55. All had suffered disrupted lives on account of their depression, which had affected their work and relationships. None was currently working, and a few had other health problems such as migraine. One member of the group was partially disabled after having two strokes.

All the participants except one had had some form of treatment for their depression. Group members had experience of drug treatments, counselling, psychotherapy and electroconvulsive therapy (ECT). They recounted a variety of negative experiences to do with gaining access to treatments, being forcibly treated and suffering from the side-effects of treatment. In general, the participants had experienced quite severe depression. Several were members of mental health groups/organisations such as Mind.

Academic specialists

The specialist reviewers included a professor of general psychiatry, a reader in psychological medicine, and a senior lecturer in psychiatry, all of whom were experts in the study of depression and its treatment.

The materials

Dealing with Depression: SmithKline Beecham
Depression: Royal College of Psychiatrists (RCP)
Overcoming Depression: Krames Communications
Understanding Depression: Hawker Publications
What Everyone Should Know about Depression: Scriptographic
Anti-Depressants: Mind
Depression Helpline: College of Health
Depression: Videos for Patients

Rankings

	Patients	Specialists
1	Scriptographic	RCP
2	Mind (1=)	Scriptographic
3	Videos for Patients	Videos for Patients
4	Hawker	Hawker
5	College of Health	College of Health
6	RCP	SmithKline Beecham
7	Krames	Krames
8	SmithKline Beecham	Mind

Summary of reviews

With the exception of the video on depression produced by Videos for Patients, these were all written materials. Patients and specialists were in broad agreement on the rankings for these materials with two exceptions: the Mind booklet was liked by patients but not by specialists, and the specialists liked the Royal College of Psychiatrists booklet but the patients did not. Patients disliked the small print size, writing style and tone of the RCP booklet although they appreciated the information it contained. Views on the Mind booklet differed within the groups, but specialists felt it was over-detailed and somewhat biased against drugs.

Specialists felt that the RCP booklet provided the most useful information for patients who wanted to be informed participants in decisions about their care, and the Scriptographic booklet, the telephone tape, and the video were also rated above average in this respect. The other materials were not felt to be particularly helpful.

> **Dealing with Depression:** SmithKline Beecham Pharmaceuticals and Healthy Alliance

Overall ratings:	Patients	6.4 (range 2–10) rank 8 (out of 8)
	Specialists	5.3 (range 5–6) rank 6

Publication date: No date on leaflet.

Address: SmithKline Beecham Pharmaceuticals, Welwyn Garden City, Hertfordshire AL7 1EY.

Description

This is a short pamphlet folded in three with three colour cartoons. Sections include: what is depression?; life events; biological causes; how depression is treated; drug therapy; length of treatment; counselling; the next six months; the first important weeks; keeping up treatment; the future.

Patients' views

This was felt to be potentially useful as a truly introductory leaflet about depression, but its lack of depth meant that follow up information would almost certainly be needed. There was some concern that the leaflet was unduly optimistic. The source of the leaflet (drug company) made several people regard it with suspicion, and it was felt by some that drugs were so over-emphasised that even if it had appeared to come from a different source they would have judged it to be biased. There was also a view that the content did not really deliver what the title had suggested it would. The focus group participants did not believe the leaflet would have helped them think about treatment choices (counselling was only mentioned as a possible complement to drugs).

There was concern that the leaflet assumed that GPs would be knowledgeable about depression and sympathetic to people suffering from it. The experiences of the focus group participants led them to believe that this was not always the case, and they criticised the leaflet for not suggesting where people might go for help if their GPs were not helpful.

The well defined structure and clear language of this leaflet were generally positively commented on, and its conciseness made it more attractive than some of the other leaflets to people for whom concentration was a problem. Opinions differed about the acceptability of the cartoons; while some welcomed the element of humour and the attempt to lighten up the subject, others strongly disliked the suggestion that depression could be made funny.

Academic specialists' views

This short pamphlet was commended by the specialists for its attractive presentation, clear language and easy style and for the fact that it managed reasonably broad coverage. However they were critical of some serious omissions, including psychological treatments, cognitive therapy, social interventions, lithium and ECT. Coverage of treatment options was considered to be biased towards antidepressants.

The pamphlet was rated highly for visual appeal, readability and style, but it received low ratings for description of the condition and its consequences and for assisting with informed choice. Some important causes of depression, for example genetic factors and physical illness, were omitted. It was criticised for failing to cover the consequences of depression, for example its effect on work and relationships.

Dealing with depression: SmithKline Beecham

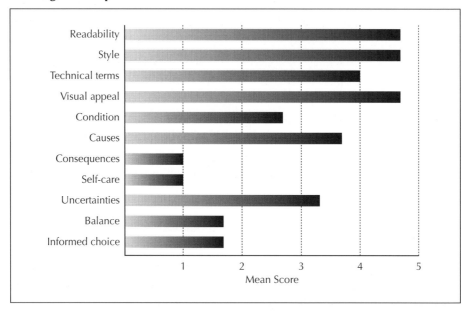

Depression: Royal College of Psychiatrists in association with Royal College of General Practitioners

Overall ratings: Patients   7.1 (range 4–9) rank 6
                       Specialists   8.0 (range 7–9) rank 1

Publication date: April 1996

Address: Royal College of Psychiatrists, 17 Belgrave Square, London SW1X 8PG.

Description

The booklet was written by one author who both suffers from and is an expert on depression, drawing on comments from the RCP's Public Education Committee and a well-known 'agony aunt'. The aim was to produce a user-friendly leaflet on depression, its treatment, symptoms, and self-help techniques. It aims to encourage people to seek help and to provide reassurance that they are not alone. Comments were sought from the RCP's Patients' and Carers' Liaison Group which includes members from the main national user and carer organisations. It was evaluated by means of a questionnaire to users. More than a million copies of the booklet have been distributed. It is currently being updated and revised for reprinting. It is intended for general use and distribution via GPs, specialists, pharmacies, health promotion and public libraries.

It is a 14-page booklet printed in two colours and illustrated with Calman cartoons. Sections include: introduction – depression; seeking help; symptoms; causes; treatment; not getting better; how to help yourself; relatives and friends; support groups and caring organisations; 'help is at hand' leaflets; defeating depression.

Patients' views

This booklet was felt to be informative, and the range of treatments covered was appreciated. Several people felt it appropriate that talking treatments were discussed before drugs. The section on ECT, however, was thought to be inappropriately reassuring: 'It makes it sound quite nice in there'.

The simple, basic suggestions in the section entitled 'How to help yourself' were deemed to be useful, and the section entitled 'Friends and family' was positively valued. The level of detail offered in the leaflet made some people suggest that it would be more useful for relatives or friends than the person with depression, at least in the early stages of their illness.

The small print, writing style and tone of the leaflet were all criticised, and put some people off reading it altogether. The tone was thought to be patronising and it was suggested that the people writing the leaflet had not really been interested in what they were doing.

Academic specialists' views

The reviewers liked this booklet for its clear account of the features, causes and treatment of depression. It was commended for including advice for relatives and carers, and information about resistant depression. They felt it contained good detail on symptoms of depression, but little on symptoms of anxiety and nothing on prevalence of depression or on genetic factors. Drug therapies and ECT were covered well, but major omissions included psychological treatments, for example cognitive therapy, psychotherapy and counselling, which one reviewer considered 'a surprising oversight'.

Reviewers had differing responses to the tone of the booklet: one said 'doesn't patronise', while another felt it was 'a little patronising, *ex cathedra*. Perhaps still a little too 'doctor knows best'-ish in style'. The cartoons were appreciated, although it was felt the text was a bit dense and could have been improved with more white spaces on the page.

Depression: Royal College of Psychiatrists

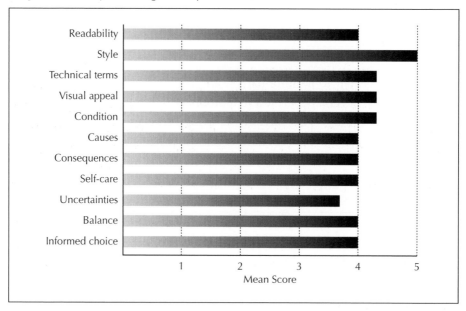

Overcoming Depression: Krames Communications

Overall ratings: Patients   6.8 (range 1–10) rank 7
                     Specialists   4.7 (range 4–5) rank 7

Publication date: 1989

Address: Krames Communications, 1100 Grundy Lane, San
                     Bruno, California 94066-3030, USA.

Description

This eight-page leaflet illustrated with full colour cartoons was produced in the USA. The leaflet carries the accreditation symbol of the American Academy of Family Physicians Foundation. It includes sections on: depression – a serious medical illness; myths that keep people down; self-assessment – is it depression?; understanding depression; a step-by-step recovery; everyone deserves to feel good.

Patients' views

Discussion of this leaflet focused mainly on the presentational style, about which opinions diverged dramatically (the divergence of opinions about presentation seemed to account for the wide range of scores given to it). Those who rated the leaflet highly found it 'very human', 'incisive', 'positive', 'bright' and 'invitingly jolly to read'. Those who disliked it described it disparagingly as 'cartoonish', 'OTT', 'Americanised' and 'gimmicky'. Some struggled to read it because they were put off by the style of presentation.

There was a view that the leaflet could help people get over the obstacle of recognising that they were depressed and deciding to consult a doctor. It was also suggested that the leaflet might be more attractive to younger people.

Academic specialists' views

The specialist reviewers were divided in their reactions to the style of this leaflet. One reviewer 'found the cartoons very offputting. The text was OK but the cartoons trivialised it. Like a comic. Can't imagine a depressed person taking it seriously.' Another said: 'Very well presented, if a little patronising in the last cartoon', while the third found it 'attractive, and interesting pictures throughout.'

The description of symptoms was highly commended by all reviewers, but there was little information on prevalence or prognosis: 'Informative, but often unclear when explaining technical terms and too limited in scope'. The leaflet provided useful information on self-help, but other information on treatment options was severely limited with no discussion of efficacy or side-effects. ECT was not mentioned at all. None of the reviewers felt this leaflet would be a useful aid to shared decision-making about treatments.

Overcoming depression: Krames Communications

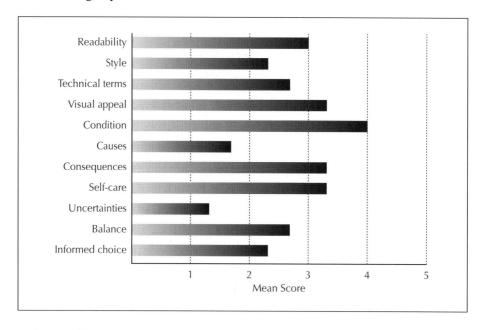

Understanding Depression: Hawker Publications Ltd sponsored by Lundbeck Ltd

Overall ratings: Patients   8.1 (range 5–10) rank 4
                     Specialists   6.3 (range 4–8) rank 4

Publication date: 1995

Address: Hawker Publications Ltd, 13 Park House, 140 Battersea Park Road, London SW11 4NB.

Description

This 16-page booklet with full colour illustrations is part of the 'Understanding Health' series. Sections include: what is depression?; what causes depression?; what it feels like; how to help a person with depression; when should we go to the doctor?; what is the medical treatment?; the good news; useful addresses.

Patients' views

The booklet was generally quite highly rated. It was considered to contain helpful and accurate information that was presented in a clear, concise way. The information about treatments, including psychotherapy and ECT, was thought to be 'honest', and it was suggested that because the leaflet was informative without being too technical, it could be useful for friends, relatives or carers. Consideration of the effects of depression on other people was particularly appreciated. On the negative side, it was suggested that the booklet might contain too much information for a sick person to take in, and that it relied heavily on GPs being knowledgeable and caring, which participants had not always found to be the case.

There was agreement that the language of the booklet made it easy to read, but other aspects of its presentation attracted some divergent views. For some people the pictures were relaxing, but for others they were depressing, gloomy or even disturbing.

Academic specialists' views

This booklet was commended for its coverage of the aetiology of depression and the description of the symptoms, but treatment options were considered to be less well covered. Specialists felt it contained detailed information on drug therapies but little on psychological treatments. They criticised it for inadequate coverage of self-help. In general it was felt to be unbalanced in its coverage of the treatment options.

Opinions differed on the presentational style, but the illustrations were disliked. 'Very well presented – avoids the patronising cartoons, but goes for meaningless art instead'. 'The photographs are dark and brooding, the text too dense, and too little white space used'.

Reviewers did not feel this booklet provided enough detail and balance to promote shared decision-making or informed treatment choices.

Understanding depression: Hawker Publications

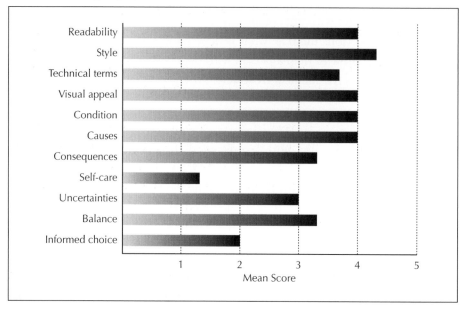

What Everyone Should Know about Depression: Scriptographic

Overall ratings: Patients   8.4 (range 6–10) rank 1=
                      Specialists   7.0 (range 7–7) rank 2

Publication date: 1995

Address: Scriptographic Publications Ltd, Channing House,
                    Butts Road, Alton, Hants GU34 1ND.

Description

This is a 16-page two-colour booklet designed for people who have concerns that they, or someone they care for, may be suffering from depression. Intended for use in primary care, it is one of a series of booklets providing information on a wide range of public health, health promotion and patient education issues. The publishers report that the format has evolved over many years of experience and evaluation.

Information sources include knowledge from relevant organisations (e.g. Mind, Depression Alliance) and published research articles. Market research was used to determine the content. Clinical experts and subject specialists were invited to evaluate the drafts and to provide supplementary material where necessary. Scriptographic's US parent company uses focus groups to identify the content and approach and they have plans to do the same in the UK.

Sections include: what is depression? depression is common in the United Kingdom; depression can affect anyone; causes of depression; symptoms of depression; the common types of depression; treatment of depression; the people who treat depression; where to get help; you can take action; learn about depression.

Patients' views

The focus group members were positively enthusiastic about this booklet, which was summed up as 'excellent', 'brilliant', and 'top of the class'. It was considered more comprehensive and informative than most other leaflets, and more useful for helping people to make informed choices about treatment. The explicit recognition that there are different forms of depression, the inclusion of information about alternative therapies, and the provision of information about the side-effects of treatments, including ECT, were particularly welcomed.

The arrangement of columns and headings was liked, and there was agreement that the leaflet was easy to read. However, the cover was felt to be uninspiring, and the quality of the paper poor. As with other booklets on depression, some people disliked the use of cartoons.

Academic specialists' views

This booklet achieved consistently high ratings from the reviewers who liked its form, content and style. 'Provides detailed and interesting information about prevalence and features of depression. Hard to fault!' There were considered to be no major omissions among the treatment options covered, although one reviewer felt the information on ECT was inaccurate and the discussion of antidepressants could have been more detailed.

Reviewers liked the simple illustrations and the clear, friendly language. In general the booklet was considered to be balanced and unbiased and as such could be a useful aid to shared decision-making.

What everyone should know about depression: Scriptographic

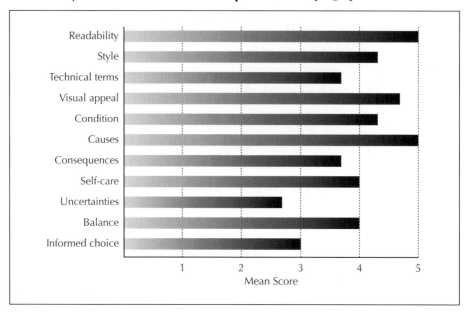

Mean Score

Making Sense of Treatment and Drugs – Anti-depressants:
Mind Publications

Overall ratings: Patients   8.4 (range 4–10) rank 1= (out of 8)
                    Specialists   4.0 (range 2–7) rank 8

Publication date: 1996

Address: Mind (National Association for Mental Health), 15–19
                    Broadway, London E15 4BQ.

Description

This 48-page booklet was designed to provide information about drug side-effects, the interactions of other psychiatric drugs with anti-depressants and about how to stop taking anti-depressants. It is distributed to those in contact with Mind groups or the Mind telephone information service. The booklet was produced in response to reports that patients were not getting full information from their doctors about adverse effects of the drugs, or the time lapse before they take effect, etc. Sources of information included psychiatry journals, the *Handbook of Psychiatric Drug Therapy*, the *British National Formulary* and the

Association of British Pharmaceutical Industries. Users were involved in its development via Mind's policy committee and a psychiatrist provided comments on drafts of the booklet, which has not been formally evaluated.

Sections include: informed consent; who suffers from depression? treatment for depression; adverse effects of antidepressants; drugs during pregnancy and breast-feeding; children and antidepressants; drug interactions; how long to stay on antidepressants; are antidepressants addictive? coming off antidepressants; tricyclic antidepressants and newer similar compounds; monoamine-oxidase inhibitor antidepressants; combination drugs; other drugs used to treat depression; selective serotonin reuptake inhibitors; further reading; index of trade and generic drug names.

Patients' views

Most focus group members rated this booklet very highly. They particularly liked the 'honest' and relatively detailed information about the pros and cons of different treatments, and the fact that an effort was being made to inform people about side-effects before they experienced them.

The booklet was judged to be well written, but its length was perceived to be a potential problem. The person who rated it lowest had felt it was too heavy and depressing, and did not finish reading it.

Academic specialists' views

The subject specialists were divided in their opinions of this booklet: one reported neutral reactions but the other two did not like it at all: 'Gives too much information on drugs. Overemphasises *dangerousness* (dangerous is a description of antidepressants which is used again and again). Recommends too low doses. There is good research evidence to indicate that higher doses are often needed'. The other reviewer was less critical, except for the following comment: 'One wonders about the wisdom of including every possible side-effect, many of which are speculative'.

The booklet achieved low ratings for style and visual appeal, with one reviewer commenting: 'No visual appeal at all – very dense, no graphics, simple regurgitation of lists'.

It was clear that the purpose of this book differed from the others reviewed here – it did not aim to promote informed choice between a range of treatment options, but simply to provide detailed information about antidepressants. Other booklets produced by Mind include one on talking treatments and one on complementary and alternative therapies.

Anti-depressants: Mind

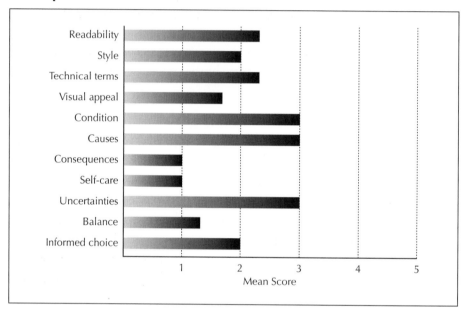

Depression Helpline: College of Health (tape nos. 089 and 298)

Overall ratings: Patients   7.7 (range 3–10) rank 5
                      Specialists   5.5 (range 5–6) rank 5

Publication date: No date on tape.

Address: College of Health, St Margaret's House, 21 Old Ford Road, London E2 9PL.

Description

This is one of a range of tapes which can be selected by callers using a Freephone number operated by the national network of health information services. The tapes can be accessed 24 hours a day, seven days a week (via a touch tone phone). They are intended to give a simple brief outline of the condition and the diagnostic tests and treatments. 'They are not designed to help people make choices, rather to make them aware that choices exist which they can discuss with their doctors' (publishers' survey).

The tape was developed according to a standard process devised by the College of Health using a variety of information sources including *Effective Health Care* bulletins and information from self-help groups or voluntary organisations. All scripts are checked by Dr Tony Smith, Associate Editor of the *BMJ*. The tape lasts five minutes. Two different versions are available.

Patients' views

Discussion about the helplines was limited. Participants who did not have touch tone telephones had been unable to get through to them, so only five members of the group had heard them. Some of the people who had heard the helpline tapes had found them informative, while others thought that they gave insufficient explanations, for example about the side-effects of drugs and what to do if these were disabling. It was suggested that the helplines might appropriately encourage some people to contact a doctor, and the emphasis on why it is important to follow instructions carefully if taking drugs for depression was appreciated.

There was a suggestion that the tapes were comforting to listen to, but rather long. The possibility of listening in privacy was seen as a positive attraction of the helpline format.

Academic specialists' views

The tape was considered to be quite informative although one reviewer commented that it was hard to absorb all the information at one go. Symptoms were felt to be well described but sleep disturbance and cognitive impairment (memory, concentration) were omitted and there was little information on prevalence. Specialists felt that most therapies were covered though not in much detail, but pointed out that there was no information on ECT or alternative therapies and nothing on self-help.

Reviewers were critical of the coverage of psychological therapies: 'Mentions cognitive therapy but far too technical and not 100 per cent accurate. Far too much about counselling (which is unproven) and too little about psychotherapy (cognitive therapy, behaviour therapy) which isn't'. Treatment risks were not covered and specialists considered that technical terms and concepts were not well explained. The information was seen as being reasonably balanced and informative.

Depression helpline: College of Health

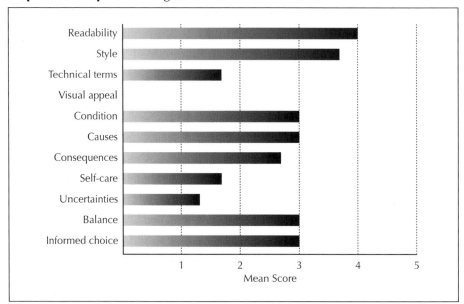

What You Really Need to Know about ... Depression: Videos for Patients, Video Arts Productions Ltd

| Overall ratings: | Patients | 8.1 (range 7–10) rank 3 |
| | Specialists | 6.7 (range 5–8) rank 3 |

| Publication date: | June 1993 |

| Address: | Videos for Patients, 18 Denbigh Close, London W11 2QH. |

Description

This is one of a series of videos edited by John Cleese and written by Dr Rob Buckman designed to give patients and their carers a full understanding of their medical condition. Contents include: what is this disease all about?; how common is it?; what are the main symptoms?; what causes it?; what is likely to happen next?; how can it be treated?; what about medication?; what is treatment like?; where can I get more information and help?

GPs lend the videos to their patients and they are also available from libraries, pharmacies, self help groups and direct mail order. Bromley Health Authority is piloting the series, seeking reviews and feedback from GPs and patients.

Patients' views

The video was generally quite highly rated, although the content was felt to be a bit basic, and there was a view that not enough information was provided about the different treatments. For example, there was no mention of ECT or hospitalisation, and the time interval between starting to take drugs and them having some effect was not explained. It was suggested that the video was a useful introduction to depression, suitable for public consumption and for people in the early stages of illness.

The video was felt to be well structured and segmented, and people liked the feeling of being talked to (not over!) by presenters who were sincere about what they were saying. Respect for the two people who featured on the video – a doctor who had experienced serious illness himself, and a successful funny man who was not without his own problems – was identified as one of the reasons why group members liked the video. It was suggested that bad actors or people who spoke in a patronising way would put people off videos completely.

The ability of the medium to convey information to people unable to read (either because of illiteracy or as a consequence of depressive illness) was appreciated. The explicit encouragement to rewind and replay sections of the video was liked by some, but others found this and the slow pace and long pauses irritating.

Academic specialists' views

The video achieved fairly high ratings from the specialists who appreciated its descriptive clarity. 'Clear and concise, assumes no prior knowledge, terms explained clearly, not depressing!'. 'Very good on symptoms, aetiology and stigma'. It was criticised for having a 'definite medical bias' and for failing to mention predisposing personality traits, self esteem as a cause rather than consequence of depression, or relationships with physical illness or alcohol problems. The omission of information about morbidity, mortality, effects on marriage and families, occupation impairment, effects on children, economic consequences was considered 'surprising'.

Most treatment options were covered with the exception of ECT, alternative therapies and self-help, but specialists felt that the risks of various treatment options were slightly underplayed. They were pleased, however, that it acknowledged the existence of uncertainties and knowledge gaps. Reviewers considered it reasonably balanced except in so far as the side-effects of tricyclic drugs were mentioned but not those of SSRIs.

The friendly and direct style was appreciated, 'conversational without being superficial' and the video was seen as a good medium for explaining difficult concepts and technical terms.

Depression: Videos for Patients

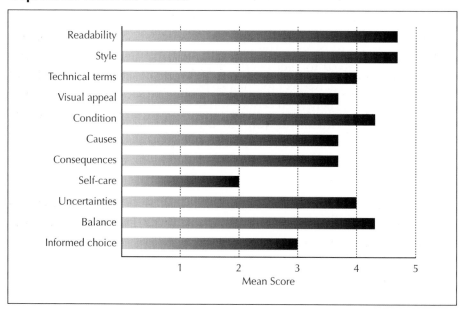

Chapter 13

Glue ear

Focus group

This focus group was difficult to recruit. It was run with just four participants, all married women and mothers of children who had had glue ear. Two of the women had worked with young children (as a nursery nurse and in play groups), and two had substantial working contact with health services (a dietician and a volunteer hospital visitor).

Three of the participants had had at least one child given surgical treatment for glue ear. One woman's three children had all had their adenoids and tonsils removed (between 10 and 20 years ago), and she had been satisfied with their treatment. Another woman's daughter had had four operations to insert grommets, which kept falling out, and a third woman's daughter had suffered perforated ear drums, possibly as a result of an operation to insert grommets. The fourth woman's 12-year-old child still had recurring glue ear. She had tried an Otovent, but had never been surgically treated. Thus it is probably fair to say that the participants between them had had more problematic experiences of glue ear and its treatment than the average parent.

Academic specialists

The specialist reviewers included the director of an MRC research unit, a professor of health services research and an ear, nose and throat consultant. All had experience of research on this condition.

The materials

Glue Ear: A guide for parents: Institute of Hearing Research
Glue Ear: A guide for parents: Hertfordshire Health Authorities
Glue Ear: Parents' leaflet: Bedfordshire Health
Glue Ear: Emis
Glue Ear: College of Health

Rankings

	Patients	*Specialists*
1	Bedfordshire	Bedfordshire
2	Hearing Research	Hearing Research
3	Emis	Hertfordshire
4	Hertfordshire	College of Health
5	College of Health	Emis

Summary of reviews

Apart from the College of Health telephone helpline, these were all written materials. Specialists and patients were agreed on which were the two best materials in this group. The leaflet produced by Bedfordshire Health was highly commended for the information it contained and for its style, tone and balance. The leaflet produced by the Institute for Hearing Research was also liked by both groups, although the lack of information about treatment risks was noted.

None of the other materials was considered by specialists to be helpful for parents wanting to make an informed choice about the options for their child.

Glue Ear: A guide for parents: Institute of Hearing Research and Hearing Research Trust

Overall ratings: Patients   7.7 (range 6–10) rank 2 (out of 5)
Specialists 6.3 (range 5–7) rank 2

Publication date: Revised February 1997, but no date on leaflet.

Address: MRC Institute of Hearing Research, University Park, Nottingham, NG7 2RD.

Description

This is a ten-page fold-out leaflet with a child's drawing in colour on the front cover. It contains one illustration – a diagram of the middle ear. Developers included the Director of the MRC Institute of Hearing Research (who was also one of the specialist reviewers) and an audiological scientist at the same Institute, together with the Director of the Hearing Research Trust. A revised edition was produced in February 1997.

According to the developers the leaflet aims to provide information to parents of children with glue ear who are at the primary care stage of consultation. 'It is not aimed at providing "evidence" to facilitate parents making an informed choice about their child's treatment, rather it aims to provide comprehensive background information about the condition, with specific guidelines for practical advice on how parents/teachers can cope during watchful waiting periods'. Users and clinicians were involved in the evaluation of early drafts.

The leaflet includes sections on: problems with hearing; changes in behaviour; signs of speech delay; difficulties in school; the ear; glue ear; ear infections; what are the effects of glue ear?; what can be done about glue ear?; if an operation is needed; how can parents help? An address is provided for further information, together with an appeal for funds for the Hearing Research Trust.

Patients' views

Overall comments about this leaflet were favourable, and it was thought to be a reasonably good general leaflet for parents encountering glue ear for the first time. The lack of information about the risks of treatment options was noted, although some felt that this need not necessarily be seen as a problem with this introductory leaflet as long as further information was provided at a later stage. It was suggested that this leaflet could be read with a child ('I wouldn't mind reading it with my child viewing it, I mean it wouldn't be threatening to a child'). The leaflet's content was felt to be more relevant for older children than toddlers.

The relatively simple language and the positive tone of the leaflet were well liked, and the bright colours were appreciated. The diagram of the ear, however, received some criticism for lack of clarity. The identification of a source of further information was appreciated, but there was some concern about the fact that money was asked for in return.

Academic specialists' views

Achieving higher than average scores in all categories other than its coverage of uncertainties, this leaflet was described as 'generally accurate and intelligible'. It was thought to provide helpful advice for parents, although one reviewer felt it could have gone further: 'It doesn't explore the difference between a hearing and a listening problem. Also, telling parents to get their child to sit near teacher assumes children sit in rows at school. Tend to be in small groups!'

Information on the causes of the problem was thought to be limited and the leaflet was criticised for perpetuating the view that glue ear can be a consequence rather than a cause of acute otitis media. It scored highly for provision of balanced information but there was not much information on hearing tests or tympanometry, and hearing aids and Otovent were omitted from the list of treatment options. One expert found it a bit patronising because it avoided mentioning risks and outcome probabilities. Another felt it failed to deal adequately with the issue of watchful waiting, and it scored only average marks for supporting informed choice.

Glue ear: a guide for parents: Institute of Hearing Research

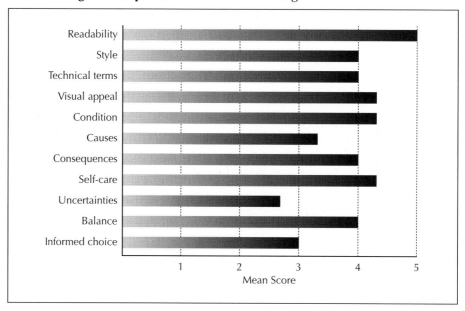

Glue Ear: A guide for parents: Hertfordshire Health Authorities

Overall ratings: Patients   6.5 (range 6–7) rank 4
                    Specialists   6.0 (range 5–7) rank 3

Publication date: May 1996

Address: Hertfordshire Health Authorities, Charter House,
                    Parkway, Welwyn Garden City, Hertfordshire AL8 6JL.

Description

This four-page two-colour leaflet contains cartoons and a diagram of the inner ear. It includes sections on: what is glue ear?; what will the doctor do about it?; what is the surgical treatment?; what is the medical treatment?; how can I help my child? The last page includes a summary of helpful things parents can do.

Patients' views

The leaflet was judged to provide some useful information about glue ear ('any information actually is useful'), and hence to be of some value to parents 'at the beginning' of their glue ear encounters. Information about the risks and benefits of treatments, however, was felt to be inadequate and the lack of practical advice (e.g. about hair washing and swimming) was criticised.

The heaviest criticisms of this leaflet focused on its perceived 'remote' clinical language and negative tone. Although it mentioned a few risks of treatment, people felt these had been expressed in 'rather an unpleasant way', with no balancing reassurance. Opinions varied about the colour of the leaflet, which was liked by some and described as 'bland' and 'depressing' by others. Some people found the lack of eyes on the illustrations disturbing.

Academic specialists' views

The leaflet scored highly for information about the condition and on self-care and for readability and style, but it was given low marks for the way in which it described the causes of the condition and treatment uncertainties.

Specialists felt it contained inaccurate information about bottle-feeding and the effectiveness of treatments and considered the information on the prognosis of different options too insufficient to be useful. They criticised the leaflet for excluding information about the complications of surgery and the benefits and risks of different treatments and for failing to state clearly the long-term consequences of the problem. The specialists did not feel it included sufficient information to help parents make informed choices about treatment.

Glue ear: a guide for parents: Hertfordshire Health Authorities

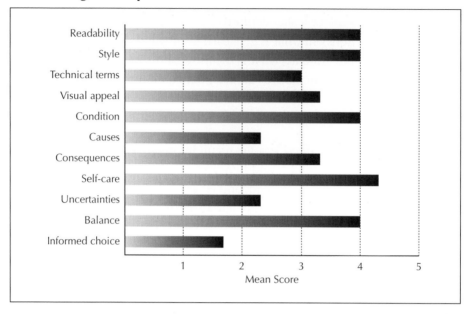

Glue Ear: Parents' leaflet: Bedfordshire Health Authority in association with the NHS Centre for Reviews and Dissemination

Overall ratings: Patients 8.6 (range 8–9) rank 1
                  Specialists 8.7 (range 7–10) rank 1

Publication date: 1996, but no date on leaflet.

Address: Bedfordshire Health Authority, Charter House, Alma Street, Luton, Beds LU1 2PL.

Description

Written by two research fellows from the NHS Centre for Reviews and Dissemination, the leaflet aims to provide people with research-based information about treatment options for children with glue ear. The content was based on a systematic review of research evidence supplemented by primary research where appropriate. A three-colour leaflet with six pages, it includes two diagrams showing the inner and outer ear. Parents and professionals were consulted during development. A small study has been undertaken to evaluate the leaflet.

Sections include: what is glue ear?; how does glue ear affect hearing?; how can we tell if your child has glue ear?; does your child need any treatment?; what about an operation?; disadvantages of surgery; what is best for my child?; what happens now? Space is provided to note down points for discussion with a doctor.

Patients' views

Most comments about this leaflet were highly favourable. The leaflet was felt to be particularly informative about surgery and treatment options, people were interested in the 'honest' section about what was not known, and the way that risks were presented 'in an informative and supportive way' was appreciated. Mention of the need to check hearing just before surgery was welcomed, but the leaflet was criticised for not including many practical tips for parents (e.g. about talking to teachers).

The presentation and tone of the leaflet were generally liked, and people appreciated the offer of more detailed information if required, the encouragement to ask questions of their doctors, and the space for jotting down questions.

Academic specialists' views

This leaflet achieved above average scores in all but one category. It was commended for providing a 'concise summary of the therapeutic rationale, risks, benefits and quality of evidence' and for providing 'accurate, evidence-based advice', but two of the specialists gave it low ratings for information about self-care. One reviewer criticised the introductory section for containing little on prevalence, remission rates and age-effects and felt it presented a conventional but possibly misleading view of pathogenesis. Another reviewer said 'It is too determined to talk down the problem. A genuinely worried parent will feel foolish and/or reject all the advice.'

The information on treatment options was commended: 'Well thought out and thorough', 'Very good account of risks and benefits'. Hearing aids were omitted from the list, but one reviewer thought this omission appropriate because 'only acceptability trials have been done and it is not as simple as some public health doctors imagine'. Most of the comments on this leaflet were positive and the leaflet was considered clear and well balanced.

Glue ear: parents' leaflet: Bedfordshire Health

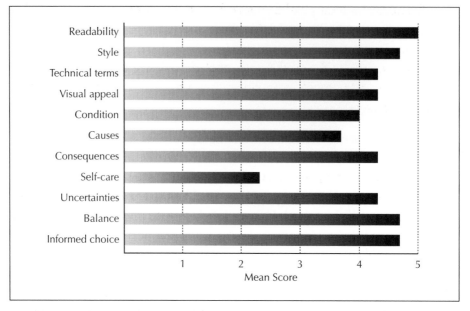

Glue Ear: EMIS Patient Information Leaflets

Overall ratings: Patients   6.8 (range 5–8) rank 3
                    Specialists   4.3 (range 4–5) rank 5

Publication date: 1996

Address: Patient Information Publications, 50 The Grove,
                    Gosforth, Newcastle upon Tyne, NE3 1NJ.

Description

This leaflet is incorporated into the clinical software package which EMIS supplies to general practices. It was written by two Newcastle GPs for a company called Patient Information Publications. The leaflets, which are revised annually, are designed to be given to a patient after a GP consultation. The glue ear leaflet aims to explain the condition to parents and to briefly discuss the treatment options. The content was based on review articles about glue ear. The views of a patient group, the British Deaf Association, have been sought and their comments will be incorporated in the revised version due out soon. Evaluation has included feedback from a patient group, a survey of GPs and a formal assessment of readability.

Printed out on two A4 sheets, the leaflet includes a description of the condition and sections on: what are the symptoms?; is it serious?; what can be done?; will the problem go away?

Patients' views

The focus group participants appreciated the fact that this leaflet gave them some useful information, but it was considered less informative than several of the other leaflets. The focus on issues relating to the child's education and learning was appreciated, but the total omission of any reference to risk in surgery was disliked.

Although the information was judged quite easy to understand, the format was considered 'boring' and several people were irked by inconsistencies in spelling.

Academic specialists' views

The specialists were critical of this leaflet which achieved low scores in all categories except for its coverage of the consequences of the condition. It was described as poorly written, poorly structured, unattractive and dull: 'The essentials are there but the presentation is amateur'. It was criticised for failing to mention the benefits of parents stopping smoking and for mistakenly assuming that children at the most prevalent age sit in rows in the school classroom.

Specialists felt it contained some inaccuracies and omissions and did not deal adequately with scientific uncertainties or risks. 'General lack of specificity about benefits. Little or no mention of risks'. The information was not considered sufficient to assist parents in making informed decisions about treatment options: 'Not presented in a way which is conducive to comparing options'.

Glue Ear: EMIS

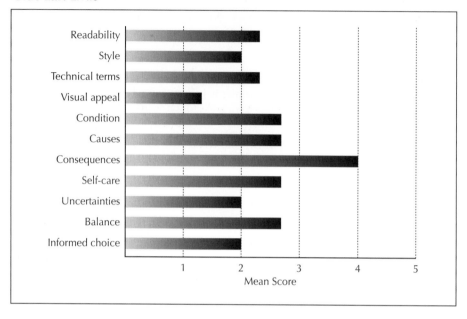

Overall ratings: Patients   6.0 (range 4–8) rank 5
                     Specialists   5.3 (range 5–6) rank 4

Publication date: October 1996

Address: College of Health, St Margaret's House, 21 Old Ford
                     Road, London E2 9PL.

Description

This is one of a range of tapes which can be selected by callers using a Freephone number operated by the national network of health information services. The tapes can be accessed 24 hours a day, seven days a week (via a touch tone phone). They are intended to give a simple brief outline of the condition and the diagnostic tests and treatments. 'They are not designed to help people make choices, rather to make them aware that choices exist which they can discuss with their doctors' (publishers' survey). This tape was devised according to a standard process developed by the College of Health using a variety of information sources, including *Effective Health Care* bulletins and information from self-help groups or voluntary organisations. All scripts are checked by Dr Tony Smith, Associate Editor of the *BMJ*. The tape lasts five minutes.

Patients' views

Although the provision of some useful information, for example about how glue ear is diagnosed and about treatment processes, was appreciated, this was perceived to be the least useful of the information materials given to the focus group participants.

Much of the discussion focused on issues relating to the tape by telephone medium. Several people had found it difficult to hear, and the problem of trying to remember what had been said was felt to be a substantial disadvantage. It was also pointed out that it was difficult to share information provided in this way, for example with a partner.

Academic specialists' views

Specialists gave the tape high scores for description of the condition and for clarity, but all other ratings were below average. Several omissions were noted among the treatment options including Otovent, hearing aids and decongestants. There was no mention of behavioural management except sitting the child at the front of the class, but it was pointed out that at the age when glue ear is most prevalent children do not sit in rows at school. The specialists disliked that fact that nothing was said about the benefits of eliminating cigarette smoke from the child's environment. There was almost no mention of uncertainties and they felt it contained insufficient information on risks and benefits of options to aid decision-making.

Specialists acknowledged that tape is more limited than visual presentation in the amount of information that can be included, but they felt that this tape provided insufficient information to support shared decision-making.

Glue Ear: College of Health

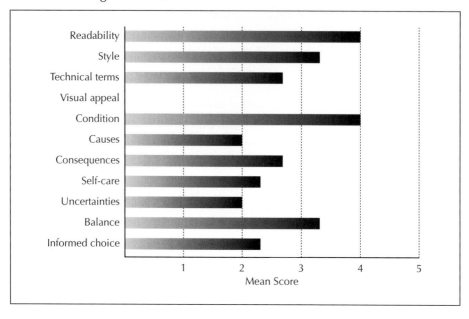

Chapter 14

High cholesterol

Focus group

This focus group included five women and three men, all of whom were middle aged or older. Three members of the group had had heart attacks (in 1979, 1985 and 1989), and another suffered from angina. Four members of the group had retired from paid employment, two for health reasons.

Four participants had become aware of high cholesterol because of their manifest heart disease. Of the other four, two had had cholesterol tests because they were aware of a family risk of heart problems, and another while undergoing check-ups for (suspected) cancer.

The focus group participants had between them a range of cholesterol levels that they had been aware of for between two and 25 years. Six members of the group reported having changed their diet in an attempt to reduce their cholesterol levels, and this had apparently been successful for two of them. At least four members of the group were taking cholesterol lowering drugs.

Academic specialists

Reviewers included a professor of epidemiology, a professor of clinical pharmacology and a university reader in epidemiology, all of whom had a special interest in the problem of high cholesterol.

The materials

Understanding Cholesterol and Heart Disease: Family Doctor publications
Why Is a Cholesterol Check Important for You Now? Merck, Sharp and Dohme (MSD)
High Blood Cholesterol: British Heart Foundation (BHF)
Prevention of Coronary Heart Disease: PatientWise
Reducing Your Cholesterol: Health Promotion Wales

Rankings

	Patients	Specialists
1	Family Doctor	Family Doctor
2	MSD	Wales
3	BHF	BHF
4	PatientWise	MSD
5	Wales	PatientWise

Summary of reviews

Two booklets, two leaflets and a factsheet were assessed. Patients and specialists were unanimous in giving highest ratings to the Family Doctor booklet, which provided detailed and comprehensive information. The MSD leaflet on cholesterol screening was seen by patients as attractive and easy to read, but specialists were concerned that it was too positive about the value of screening. Patients were divided about the leaflet produced by Health Promotion Wales, which focused on dietary change rather than cholesterol-lowering medication. Specialists agreed that it overstated the effects of dietary change, but they liked it nevertheless, giving it high ratings for promoting self-care. The British Heart Foundation booklet was long and reasonably informative, but its style was considered dense and too technical. Specialists felt some of the information it contained was out of date or inaccurate. The PatientWise factsheet was considered to be too brief to be really useful to patients needing practical advice.

The specialists considered that only the Family Doctor booklet and the Health Promotion Wales leaflet provided information which would be helpful for patients wanting to make an informed choice about treatment options.

Understanding Cholesterol and Heart Disease: Family Doctor Publications Ltd in association with the British Medical Association

---

Overall ratings:	Patients	9.1 (range 7–10) rank 1 (out of 5)
	Specialists	8.0 (range 7–9) rank 1

Publication date: 1995

Address: Family Doctor Publications Ltd, 10 Butchers Row, Banbury OX16 8JH.

Description

A 60-page booklet designed to provide detailed information on the working of the heart and circulatory system, it explains heart disease and cholesterol as a risk factor and how to control it. Written by Professor Barry Lewis and edited by Dr Tony Smith, ex- Deputy Editor of the *BMJ*, the booklet is amply illustrated with full colour drawings. It is sold through pharmacies at £2.49.

The nine chapters are headed: introduction; what goes wrong; causes of heart attack; understanding lipids; high cholesterol – lowering the risk; treating a high cholesterol level; in summary; useful addresses; index.

The publishers report that this booklet is now considered overly technical and out of date as regards lipid lowering drugs, and has since been replaced.

Patients' views

This booklet was highly rated by all the participants, who appreciated the comprehensive and detailed information. The person who rated it lowest had thought it 'very good', but marked it down because 'it wasn't for quick reading'. The contents, index and summary had been helpful, and the participants were keen to keep the booklet for reference purposes. It was thought to be intended more for people who knew they had a high cholesterol level than for other members of the public.

Academic specialists' views

In general the reviewers liked this booklet which was commended for its presentation, readable style and detailed content. 'A pleasing booklet that would encourage reading and keeping.'

It was seen as balanced and generally accurate, although it was criticised for promoting cholesterol testing without mentioning the possible drawbacks and for inaccurate information on stress and socio-economic factors. Detailed information on diet was included but specialists were critical of the fact that it did not mention the disappointing effect of dietary change on cholesterol levels. The information on statins was felt to be slightly out of date and the booklet was criticised by one of the reviewers for overstating the efficacy of resins and fibrates. Nevertheless it achieved above average scores for all ratings.

Understanding cholesterol and heart disease: Family Doctor Publications

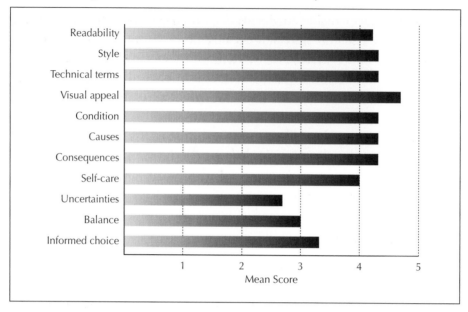

Why Is a Cholesterol Check Important for You Now? Merck, Sharp and Dohme Ltd

Overall ratings: Patients   8.4 (range 4–10) rank 2
                    Specialists   3.7 (range 2–6) rank 4

Publication date: No date on leaflet.

Address: Merck Sharp & Dohme Ltd, Hertford Road,
                    Hoddesdon, Hertfordshire EN11 9BU.

Description

This is a fold-out leaflet without illustrations. Sections are headed: where does cholesterol come from?; what is meant by high cholesterol?; what causes excess cholesterol?; what can I do about it?; what is saturated fat?; what sort of foods should I cut down?; what else can I do?; is cholesterol the only factor that might contribute to coronary heart disease?; if you have had a heart attack, angina or similar heart problems – however long ago – it is important to know your cholesterol level.

Patients' views

This leaflet was very highly rated by all but two members of the group. It was widely perceived to be an attractive document, well laid out and easy to read. The 'preliminary preventive advice' on healthy living was generally thought to be good, and the focus group members (who were all convinced of the importance of blood cholesterol testing) felt the leaflet answered the question posed in its title.

Of the people who gave the leaflet lower ratings, one thought that if it convinced people to ask their GP for a cholesterol test, the GP might not be willing to oblige. The other person disliked the leaflet because it 'came across to me as a commercial for a pharmaceutical company'.

Academic specialists' views

This leaflet is intended to promote cholesterol screening and it was criticised for providing very little additional information. Specialists were concerned that it did not explain the small contribution of cholesterol to total coronary heart disease risk and that other risk factors were only mentioned in passing, for example smoking. They pointed out that some technical terms were not explained – for example, angina. Diet was mentioned as a treatment option, but exercise was not. Reviewers were surprised that cholesterol-lowering drugs were not covered, despite the fact that the leaflet was produced by a drug company which produces these products.

The leaflet was considered attractive, 'short, clear, pleasing to the eye', but one reviewer was concerned that it would lead to some people being screened inappropriately.

Why is a cholesterol check important for you now? Merck, Sharp and Dohme

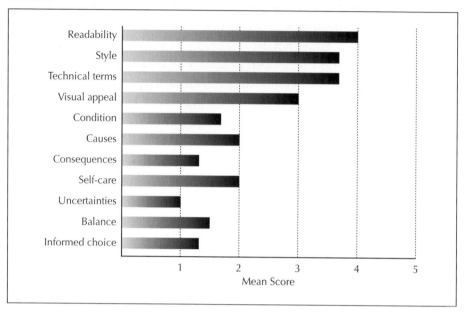

High Blood Cholesterol: British Heart Foundation

Overall ratings:	Patients	7.7 (range 6–9) rank 3
	Specialists	5.0 (range 4–6) rank 3

Publication date: October 1995

Address: British Heart Foundation, 14 Fitzhardinge Street, London W1H 4DH.

Description

This is a 24-page booklet illustrated with black and white diagrams and cartoons including the following sections: high blood cholesterol – introduction; cholesterol and other blood fats; when does your blood cholesterol level matter?; measurement of blood cholesterol and other blood fats and what the results mean; the blood cholesterol lowering diet; when can blood cholesterol-lowering medication help?; blood cholesterol lowering medication; familial hypercholesterolaemia; detection of high blood cholesterol; the work of the British Heart Foundation.

Patients' views

Participants thought that this lengthy booklet was only likely to be picked up and read by people who knew they had a problem with high blood cholesterol or heart disease and who were motivated to find out more. Several people noted that it was 'informative' and 'covered a lot', and that, in contrast with some other leaflets, it did mention the possibility of side-effects of medication, but it was thought to lack detail on the side-effects of drugs. The information about diet was liked by some but found confusing by others.

Opinions varied about the ease with which the booklet could be read. Some people found it 'too technical' and several had had difficulties understanding one of the graphs.

All the focus group members considered the British Heart Foundation to be an authoritative source. The sources of further information were appreciated.

Academic specialists' views

This booklet was long and detailed but reviewers disliked its style: 'Dense, too detailed, too technical, poorly set out, high reading age'. Despite its length there were some important omissions, including general information about heart disease, atheroma, smoking and other causes of heart disease. Reviewers felt it contained too little on what cholesterol is, including its chemistry, and thought it did not give a clear account of the interaction between diet and genetic factors, on the risk of death, or on the extent to which risk can be changed by diet or drugs.

The information on drug therapy was considered out of date in that the benefits of statins were underestimated and those of resins and fibrates over-stated and the benefits of aspirin and other drugs for secondary prevention were not mentioned. The drawbacks of cholesterol testing, for example the 'labelling' phenomenon and 'worried well' effects, were not discussed, and attention was not drawn to the limited efficacy of dietary changes.

One reviewer considered that the booklet was 'not concise, in that for its length it doesn't say a lot more than the leaflets'.

High blood cholesterol: British Heart Foundation

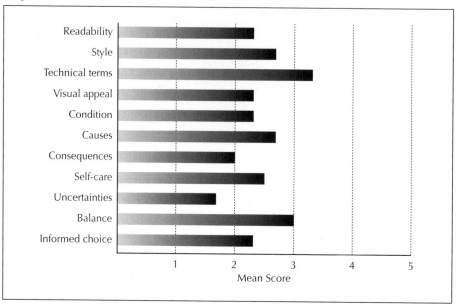

	Mean Score
Readability	
Style	
Technical terms	
Visual appeal	
Condition	
Causes	
Consequences	
Self-care	
Uncertainties	
Balance	
Informed choice	

Prevention of Coronary Heart Disease: PatientWise, John Wiley and Sons

Overall ratings:	Patients	6.6 (range 5–10) rank 4
	Specialists	3.3 (range 2–6) rank 5

Publication date: 1995

Address: PatientWise, John Wiley & Sons Ltd, 1 Oldlands Way, Bognor Regis, West Sussex, PO22 9SA.

Description

This factsheet is part of a set covering many common conditions intended to be given to patients by their GPs or hospital consultants. The latest version is designed to be accessed via Healthpoint outlets and in public libraries. It can be photocopied from a loose-leaf volume or printed out from a software version. The information on coronary heart disease was written by Dr S. Joseph, a consultant cardiologist, and Dr Peter Wise, one of the editors of PatientWise.

The sheet has been updated since it was reviewed and the new version became available in March 1997. Patients were consulted in developing the factsheet which was tested in a cardiac clinic. The format complies with Hellman's 'defined questions'. All three editors of PatientWise (a physician, a GP and a lay editor) reviewed the leaflet, and its readability level was assessed using the Gunning Fog Index. An evaluation of the PatientWise information system was published in the *Journal of the Royal Society of Medicine* (vol 89, Oct 1996, pp. 557–60).

Patients' views

Discussion of this leaflet was lost due to a problem with the tape. Individual participants' written comments (prepared prior to the focus group) were cautiously favourable about its content ('It was good as far as it goes'; 'A very, very basic article – useful as a start'). However, one person pointed out that if the leaflet was to be given to people who already had a heart condition, then it probably did not go into enough detail.

Comments about presentation were more openly critical. The leaflet was described as 'boring' and 'badly presented'. The line length was thought to be too long.

Academic specialists' views

The specialist reviewers were divided in their assessment of this leaflet, one considering it reasonably good given the limits of its length and scope, but another thinking it too brief to be useful: 'I think a large population already know what is in this. Those who do not know are not likely to be tempted to read it. If they did, they would not be much further forward as regards practical advice.'

It was criticised for its failure to cover cholesterol-lowering drugs and screening, and for omitting information on quantifying the risk of death and on the extent to which this could be modified by dietary change. One reviewer considered the dietary information inaccurate. Another particularly disliked the style and tone of the leaflet: 'Dull, unappetising, slightly censorious.'

Prevention of coronary heart disease: PatientWise

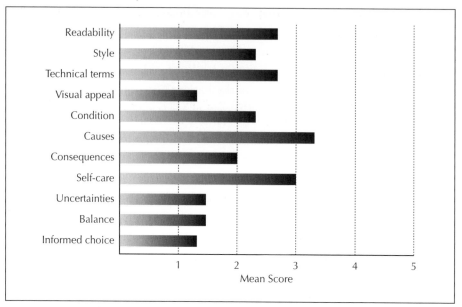

Reducing Your Cholesterol: Health Promotion Wales

Overall ratings: Patients   6.0 (range 2–9) rank 5
                       Specialists   6.3 (range 5–7) rank 2

Publication date: 1992

Address: Health Promotion Authority for Wales, Ffynnon-las, Ty
                       Glas Avenue, Llanishen, Cardiff CF4 5DZ.

Description

This is a fold-out leaflet illustrated with full-colour photographs of fish, bread,
fruit and vegetables containing sections on: what is cholesterol?; how does too
much cholesterol get into your blood?; what if my blood cholesterol is high?;
do high cholesterol levels and heart attacks always go together?; should I
worry?; how high is high?; how can I reduce my blood cholesterol?; what about
my weight?; taking exercise; what about smoking?; when can I expect my
cholesterol to start falling?; what happens if my cholesterol level doesn't come

down?; how to cut down on fat; some menu suggestions; can I eat eggs?; is oily fish good for me?; can pulses help me?; how healthy are 'health bars'?; what about vegetable oil?; useful information.

Patients' views

Participants' opinions about this leaflet were quite divided, with some liking it because it was easy to understand and 'to the point' while others criticised it for not containing enough information. As far as content was concerned, the clear, practical advice about diet and the inclusion of a sample menu were generally seen as positive features. However, the leaflet was criticised for concentrating unduly on diet and implying 'that's all you need to do'. Participants observed that it did not encourage monitoring of blood cholesterol levels, lacked advice about what to do if dietary measures were unsuccessful, and did not cover cholesterol-reducing medication.

Some people found the cover of the leaflet attractive and 'attention grabbing'. On the inside, however, the text was felt to be too small, and there was some agreement with the view that the illustration efforts had been a bit excessive: 'There's no need to put these fancy bits in there, it's information you want'.

Academic specialists' views

The subject specialists considered this an attractive leaflet, rating it high for readability, style and visual appeal. However they thought that its brevity meant it was insufficiently comprehensive and several important issues were felt to have been omitted. For example, there was almost no information on what coronary heart disease is, nothing on atheroma and nothing on genetic factors; no information was included on risk of death from heart disease and there was no information on cholesterol-lowering drugs.

The information about cholesterol testing was criticised: 'It doesn't acknowledge that cholesterol testing is a poor screening test.' The main emphasis of the leaflet is on dietary change, but reviewers felt it overstated the effects of dietary change on cholesterol levels and failed to provide information on the fat content of different foods.

Reducing your cholesterol: Health Promotion Wales

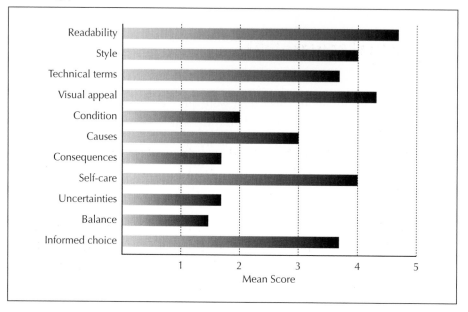

Chapter 15

Hip replacement

Focus group

The focus group comprised six women and one man whose ages ranged from late 40s to late 60s. Their hip problems were caused by developmental deformities (two women) and osteoarthritis.

Two people had not yet had a hip replacement operation; three had had one and two had had more than one total hip replacement. One person had had some post-operative problems, and one person had had an accident and acquired an infection that affected the hip after the replacement operation.

Academic specialists

Reviewers included: a university reader in orthopaedics, a professor of public health, and a consultant orthopaedic surgeon.

The materials

A New Hip Joint: Arthritis and Rheumatism Council (ARC)
The Total Hip Replacement Operation: Royal College of Surgeons (RCS)
Your Guide to the Pre-Operative and Post-Operative Management of Total Hip Replacement: DePuy
Hip Replacement: PPP Healthcare
Hip Replacement: College of Health

Rankings

	Patients	*Specialists*
1	RCS	RCS
2	DePuy	College of Health
3	College of Health	DePuy
4	PPP Healthcare	PPP Healthcare
5	ARC	ARC

Summary of reviews

The materials included two booklets, two factsheets and a telephone helpline. Patients and specialists largely agreed on the relative rankings of these materials. The Royal College of Surgeons booklet was highly appreciated by both groups for its clarity and comprehensiveness, although it did not discuss alternatives to surgical treatment. The telephone helpline was found to be quite useful, but some callers found it inaudible in parts. Patients were more enthusiastic than specialists about the DePuy booklet. Neither group liked either of the other two leaflets.

None of these materials received positive scores for promoting shared decision-making. There was an assumption by one of the specialist reviewers that choice was irrelevant for this condition, but others felt that patients might want to consider whether or when to undergo surgery and the options when it came to rehabilitation. Some patients might also want to know about different types of surgical procedure and prosthesis.

A New Hip Joint – The total hip replacement operation: Arthritis and Rheumatism Council for Research

---

Overall ratings: Patients   5.4 (range 3–7) rank 5 (out of 5)

Specialists   3.7 (range 2–6) rank 5

Publication date: No date on leaflet.

Address: Arthritis and Rheumatism Council, Copeman House, St Mary's Court, St Mary's Gate, Chesterfield, Derbyshire S41 7TD.

Description

Written by a surgeon with the help of an editorial panel of around ten professionals and lay readers, this brief leaflet is intended for anyone considering hip replacement and their carers. The leaflets are promoted to the general public and to GPs and others. A readers' panel of people with arthritis was asked to provide comments and to complete a standard questionnaire to evaluate the leaflet. A revised version of the leaflet was due to be published in January 1998.

The ten-page fold-out leaflet contains sections on: no hurry; the new joint; before the operation; after the operation; complications; don't overdo it; operation results; more information; the ARC; you can help; message from Sebastian Coe; help us improve our service.

Patients' views

Apart from one person who thought it might be useful for 'people who don't want too many details', this leaflet was not considered helpful even as an introductory guide and participants had few positive comments to offer about it. It was described as 'very poor', 'vague' and 'verbose without imparting information'. Several of the group members disputed the accuracy of both the information presented about post-operative care and the advice about returning to work and coping on a day-to-day basis. More than one participant thought the information was out of date. The inclusion of an address from which further information could be obtained was seen as a positive feature.

The tone of the leaflet was generally disliked because it was patronising, and the overall presentation attracted only negative comments.

People were disappointed that the Arthritis and Rheumatism Council had not produced a better leaflet, and in response to a question about whether the leaflet would be useful for anybody, one woman said 'It's useful for the Arthritis and Rheumatism Council because I feel the leaflet is aimed at publicising them and asking for donations – it isn't really there to impart information'.

Academic specialists' views

This leaflet achieved low scores in all categories from reviewers who criticised its content and presentation: 'Outdated. Lacks essential detail. Inaccurate. No idea about the customary management of hip replacement in 1997. Poor layout. Poor diagrams'; 'Incomplete, incorrect names, much material absent, much irrelevant, poor illustrations'. Information on self-care was considered inadequate, with too little information on the practical issues. One reviewer criticised the leaflet for making many inaccurate assertions: 'There is simply no evidence for what they say. Nil on sex, driving, gardening, swimming'. Responses to the tone of the leaflet were conflicting: 'Patronising'; 'Concise'; 'Friendly and conversational'.

The leaflet was criticised for containing almost no coverage of alternatives to surgery apart from a brief reference to 'tablets to reduce the pain' and for omitting information about arthrodesis, osteotomy, physiotherapy, NSAIDS, sticks, revisions. The discussion of hip replacement surgery was considered insufficient to promote shared decision-making: 'It's very cursory and condensed. Certainly insufficient for someone to weigh up the costs and benefits'. 'This is an unctuous document. Doctor knows best. This document would be best dated for the 1950s'.

A new hip joint: Arthritis and Rheumatism Council

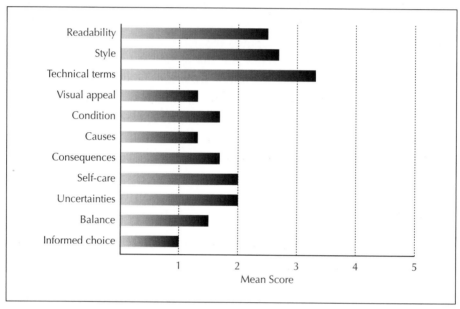

The Total Hip Replacement Operation: The Royal College of Surgeons of England

Overall ratings:	Patients	9.3 (range 8–10) rank 1
	Specialists	8.5 (range 8–9) rank 1

Publication date: 1994

Address: The Surgical Audit Unit, The Royal College of Surgeons of England, 35/43 Lincoln's Inn Fields, London WC2A 3PN.

Description

Designed to be read prior to the first outpatient appointment following referral for hip replacement, this booklet was written by staff of the Royal College of Surgeons audit unit in collaboration with two surgeons. It aims to provide detailed information about the treatment and hospital stay. According to the developers, the information sources included a review of the literature and interviews with patients about their information needs. A wide range of health professionals and consumer groups was consulted during the preparation of the booklet and a patient survey was conducted to test the design and content of various drafts, the results of which have been published in a RCS report. A revised version of the booklet is in preparation.

The 42-page booklet is amply illustrated with full colour drawings. Sections include: how you can best use this booklet; your hip joints; the treatment of arthritis; about the hospital stay; before the operation; how will I manage in the days following my operation?; adapting to life with my new hip; if I have any questions or comments; for more information. It contains two blank pages for patients' notes.

Patients' views

This booklet was given high ratings and spoken of favourably by all focus group members, who generally agreed that they would like to receive it before their operation, and preferably in time for them to influence the decision about whether and when they would have a hip replacement operation. The explicit aim of the booklet to 'guide you in the decisions you will make about yourself with your GP and surgeon' was recognised.

The participants noted that the booklet contained little information about self-help, but acknowledged that this was not its main aim. The inclusion of information about risks as well as benefits was appreciated

The clear structure and layout of the booklet, and the concise, readable text were all appreciated. It was also liked because it 'doesn't talk down to you' and is not 'frightening'.

Some people said they had confidence in the booklet because it was produced by the Royal College of Surgeons.

Academic specialists' views

The reviewers praised most aspects of this booklet which achieved high scores in most categories: 'Very comprehensive, good production, excellent graphics'. The booklet was felt to contain 'about as much detail as most people could handle'. The pictures were commended as was the direct and friendly tone of the language. Specialists felt it contained good clear anatomical diagrams and the drawings of patients were felt to be both reassuring and a helpful way of finding your way around the booklet.

One reviewer commented that the death rate given is an order of magnitude wrong, and another claimed that the survival curve was a poor representation of the truth since 50 per cent of hips are significantly painful ten years after the replacement operation.

The booklet is aimed at patients who have already decided to undergo the operation, so it does not discuss diagnosis or alternative treatments, for example medical therapy, watchful waiting, or physiotherapy, nor does it cover the problem of choice of implant or cemented vs. cementless prosthesis, or the issue of who carries out the surgery, i.e. relative experience, supervision, etc. 'This is this booklet's main failing'.

The total hip replacement operation: Royal College of Surgeons

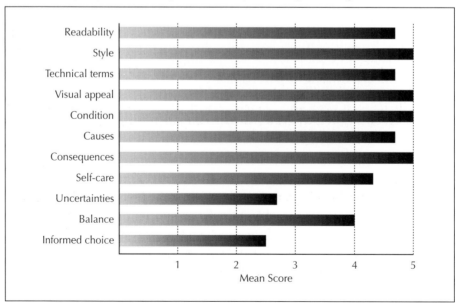

Your Guide to the Pre-Operative and Post-Operative Management of Total Hip Replacement: DePuy International Ltd

Overall ratings: Patients   8.3 (range 6–10) rank 2
                      Specialists   5.3 (range 4–7) rank 3

Publication date: No date on booklet.

Address: DePuy International Ltd, St Anthony's Road,
                      Leeds LS11 8DT.

Description

A 36-page booklet illustrated with two-colour line drawings, this was written by a physiotherapist with input from an orthopaedic surgeon, an occupational therapist, a specialist nurse and patients at an orthopaedic hospital. The following sections are included: introduction; what is total hip replacement?; what happens before the operation?; on the day of the operation; after the operation; four basic precautions; rehabilitation; getting in and out of bed; walking; getting in and out of chairs; stairs; daily activity; getting in and out of the bath; showering and dressing; preparing for leaving hospital; general household activities; helpful hints on leaving hospital; a short list of do's and don'ts; looking forward; notes.

Patients' views

This booklet was given favourable ratings by all the focus group members. They commented that it did not cover arthritis as a condition and provided little detail about the operation itself, but appreciated the emphasis on rehabilitation and how to carry out daily activities post-operatively. The booklet was seen as potentially a useful follow-on to complement the Royal College of Surgeons booklet, which was needed pre-decision or at least pre-operatively.

Although the information about rehabilitation was appreciated, several people disputed some of the advice given and noted that it conflicted with advice they had received from health professionals involved in their care. The diagrams were broadly felt to be clear and helpful, but some people had found a few of them difficult to follow. Even if the precise advice was disputed, there was a view that this booklet provided a useful guide to the kind of things that should be discussed with health care professionals.

There was little discussion of the language used and presentation of the booklet, but the comments that were made were favourable: 'Large bold print, easy to read and understand'.

Academic specialists' views

The specialist reviewers were quite critical of this booklet, although it was seen by one reviewer at least as providing helpful information about rehabilitation after surgery. It was seen as being useful in relation to the main things that will concern a patient after surgery, i.e. the various physical functions and the need to steadily recover them. However, this information was criticised by another reviewer who denounced it as 'out of date, anecdotal, not evidence-based'. The tone was criticised for being prescriptive and didactic, admitting of no uncertainties: 'Full of negative imperatives – "DO NOT"; "DO NOT ATTEMPT IT BY YOURSELF" – why in heaven's name not? Ridiculous!'.

Specialists were divided in their response to the illustrations. One reviewer thought the diagrams were 'excellent', while another thought they were 'poor': 'The chap sitting on the lavatory has got his trousers on!'.

Specialists pointed out that the booklet provided very little information about the conditions for which THR is performed and there was no discussion of alternative treatments, i.e. watchful waiting, osteotomy, arthrodesis, medical management. For this reason they felt it lacked balance and did nothing to promote informed choice.

Hip replacement: DePuy

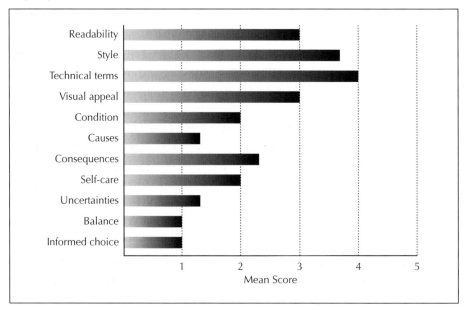

Hip Replacement: PPP Healthcare Health Information Line Fact Sheet

Overall ratings: Patients   6.3 (range 4–10) rank 5
                   Specialists   4.0 (range 1–6) rank 4

Publication date: No date on factsheet.

Address: PPP Healthcare Ltd, PPP House, Vale Road, Tunbridge
                   Wells, Kent TN1 1BJ.

Description

The factsheet consists of five sides of A4 stapled together with no illustrations. Sections include: what is a hip replacement? why is it done? how is it done? what types of artificial hips are used? what happens after surgery? what are the risks? will the operation be successful? how long will the replacement last? are there any new developments? are there self help strategies? where can I obtain further information? information sources.

Patients' views

Most of the participants were critical of this leaflet and gave it low ratings. They felt it lacked background information, and did not provide enough detail about hospital procedures and how to manage day to day activities post-operatively. The leaflet made a few points that they appreciated that had not been made in other leaflets, for example about the benefits of losing even a small amount of weight, and about the risks of blood clots.

Although the complete lack of diagrams was disliked by most focus group members, the one person who rated this leaflet highly (who had not yet had a hip replacement) liked it precisely because it did not contain any off-putting pictures, and described the leaflet as 'short, sharp and informative'. The other group members disagreed vigorously with this view.

The focus group members were scathing about the fact that the leaflet had been produced by PPP Healthcare. One person caricatured the leaflet as saying 'everything could go wrong, all the time, everywhere' because PPP were 'covering their backs' in case anything went wrong.

Academic specialists' views

This brief factsheet was not particularly well received by the specialist reviewers who found it boringly presented and patronising in tone. Information about arthritis was seen as too schematic and condensed, alternative treatment options were not discussed, and information about lifestyle changes to optimise post-operative recovery was considered much too sketchy to be useful. However they felt the risks and benefits of total hip replacement were reasonably well covered.

Two of the reviewers thought the language used was much too technical. This leaflet was not thought to be much use for patients wanting to participate in decisions about their care.

Hip replacement: PPP Healthcare

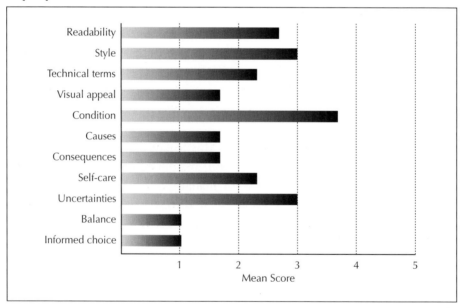

Hip Replacement: Which Healthline in association with College of Health

Overall ratings: Patients   6.4 (range 2–10) rank 3
                      Specialists   6.3 (range 5–8) rank 2

Publication date: January 1995

Address: College of Health, St Margaret's House, 21 Old Ford
                      Road, London E2 9PL.

Description

This is one of a range of tapes which can be selected by callers using a Freephone number operated by the national network of health information services. The tapes can be accessed 24 hours a day, seven days a week (via a touch tone phone). They are intended to give a simple brief outline of the condition and the diagnostic tests and treatments. 'They are not designed to help people make choices, rather to make them aware that choices exist which they can discuss with their doctors' (developer's survey).

This tape was developed according to a standard process devised by the College of Health using a variety of information sources including *Effective Health Care* bulletins and information from self-help groups or voluntary organisations. All scripts are checked by Dr Tony Smith, Associate Editor of the *BMJ*. The tape lasts five minutes. The hip replacement tape was due for revision in May 1997.

Patients' views

One person had been unable to get through to the helpline, and a couple of others had had difficulty hearing parts of the tape. The ratings varied substantially, but discussions suggested that the people who had given lower ratings had done so at least partly because of audibility problems and because it was difficult to remember everything that was said. The helpline medium did not allow them to go back and check things or just listen to small parts again.

The tape was thought to be comprehensive, with descriptions of the amount and duration of pain that matched people's experiences and useful information about sex that was not included in some of the other materials. The inclusion of further sources of information and advice was appreciated. The language and voice were described as 'reassuring'.

Academic specialists' views

This tape achieved high scores for clarity and comprehensibility, for its description of the conditions for which total hip replacement is performed and for information about self-care. Specialists commended it for providing helpful information on post-surgical recovery: 'Unlikely you will wear your hip out by over-use (Good). Good advice on sex and driving'. Alternative treatment options were not discussed and reviewers suggested some of the information was out of date: 'Advocates cementless hips – this is wrong. Lots of rubbish on thromboprophylaxis – no evidence for this'.

One reviewer found the tape inaudible in parts but another found it 'clear, easy to follow and in very accessible language'.

Hip replacement: College of Health

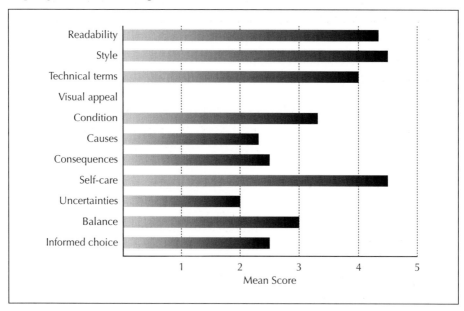

Chapter 16

Infertility

Focus group

The focus group comprised four married women. Two were 23, one 26 and the other 36 years old. One woman had one child, and the others remained childless after between two and nine and a half years of trying for a baby.

All four women had undergone a range of tests, and two were known to have polycystic ovary syndrome. One woman was undergoing fertility treatment under the care of her general practitioner and the others had attended, or were attending, specialist units.

One woman who had been receiving treatment for fertility problems for a long time acknowledged that it was difficult for her to assess introductory level information materials because she had acquired a lot of knowledge and experience over the years.

Academic specialists

Two of the three specialists who originally agreed to review the materials did not return their review forms, so the opinions reported here are from the one remaining reviewer, a professor of obstetrics and gynaecology.

The materials

Infertility: Women's Health Concern (WHC)
So You Want to Have a Baby?: Serono Laboratories
Infertility: Women's Health
Female Infertility, Male Infertility: PPP Healthcare
NURTURE: Nottingham University

Rankings

	Patients	Specialists
1	Serono	NURTURE
2	Women's Health (1=)	Women's Health

3   NURTURE   PPP Healthcare
4   WHC   WHC
5   PPP Healthcare   Serono

Summary of reviews

All materials reviewed on infertility were written as opposed to audio or video. The patients gave high ratings to all except the PPP factsheets, but the specialist was quite critical of all of them. The Serono booklet was highly praised by the patients, but the specialist felt it contained out-of-date, inaccurate and misleading information. He preferred the Women's Health leaflet which the patients also liked, although its presentation was not particularly attractive. The package of materials produced by Nottingham University was designed to advertise the NURTURE clinic and not specifically to provide general information about treatment options. Only the Women's Health leaflet received high marks for promoting informed choice, but it contained too little detail to be really useful. The NURTURE package also contained some useful information. All the other materials were considered too limited to be helpful to patients who wanted to understand the full range of options facing them.

Infertility: Women's Health Concern

Overall ratings: Patients   7.0 (range 6–8) rank 4
                       Specialist   3.0 rank 4

Publication date: 1992

Address: Women's Health Concern Ltd, PO Box 1629,
                       London W8 6AU.

Description

These two fold-out leaflets on male and female infertility each contain one illustration (an anatomical drawing). Section headings include: what are the causes of infertility?; where can I get help?; sperm test; basal temperature charts; other tests of ovulation; the post-coital test; the hysterosalpingram; laparoscopy and hydrotubation; ovulation induction; tubal surgery; in-vitro fertilisation (IVF); gamete intrafallopian transfer (gift); artificial insemination; the treatment of the male/female; counselling; the future; further reading; information about Women's Health Concern. The leaflet was written by a senior registrar at Queen Charlotte's and Chelsea Hospital, London.

Patients' views

On the positive side, these short leaflets were felt to contain useful and accessible introductory information. There was some concern, however, that they went 'too far ahead' for introductory leaflets, mentioning a whole sequence of rather 'scary' interventions that might be given 'if basic treatments did not work'.

The tone of the leaflets was criticised for being 'condescending', 'too clinical' and lacking 'the human touch'. One woman suggested 'It reads to me more as if it was aimed at somebody who just wanted to know than somebody who was actually going to need to know'.

The covers were generally agreed to be uninspiring, and the 'old-fashioned' look led several participants to anticipate that the leaflets were not going to tell them much.

Academic specialist's views

These leaflets cover most of the treatment choices for both male and female infertility with the exception of gonadotrophin drugs, but provide very little detail on any of them. The specialist reviewer was not impressed by their visual appeal, but felt the language used was factual and clearly expressed. He felt the women's leaflet was better than the men's one. The epidemiological information was considered inaccurate in parts, and the factsheets were criticised for failing to include self-help information and for not providing sufficient information on risks and uncertainties. In general the specialist reviewer felt these leaflets did little to promote shared decision-making.

Infertility: Women's Health Concern

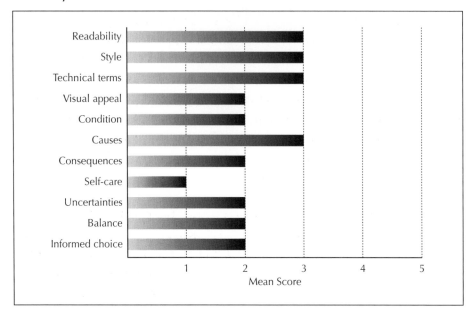

Mean Score

So You Want to Have a Baby?: Serono Laboratories (UK) Ltd

Overall ratings: Patients   8.8 (range 8–10) rank 1=
                     Specialist   2.0 rank 5

Publication date: 1992

Address: Serono Laboratories (UK) Ltd, 99 Bridge Road East,
                     Welwyn Garden City, Hertfordshire AL7 1BG.

Description

This 64-page booklet is illustrated with two-colour diagrams. It includes: preface; introduction; ovulation and fertilisation; seeking professional advice; history and examination; infertility investigations; infertility treatments; male infertility; treatment; endometriosis; tubal surgery; in-vitro fertilisation; 'unexplained' infertility treatment options; premature menopause and ovarian failure; adoption; coming to terms with your infertility; useful addresses; glossary of terms.

Patients' views

The content of this booklet was praised by the participants, with the comprehensiveness and depth of the information provided being particularly appreciated. One woman said: 'It's almost like an encyclopaedia of infertility'. It had told some of the women things they hadn't known before. The inclusion of a glossary and of temperature charts with explanations of how they were used was particularly liked. The participants varied in their views of the section on 'Coming to terms with infertility', but generally agreed that this information was less appropriate for women who were early on in the process of seeking help for fertility problems.

Although the booklet was judged easy to read, there were felt to be some shortcomings in presentation. The title was generally felt to be patronising. Several participants disliked the cover illustration of a mother, father and baby, all with no faces, although for at least one woman this encapsulated the way patients were treated by the medical profession as 'faceless nobodies'.

Academic specialist's views

Despite the length of this booklet and the quantity of detailed information it contains, the specialist reviewer was highly critical, giving it low ratings for most features. He felt it was too detailed and technical with a slightly patronising tone. 'Too much information based on too little evidence. Complicates rather than clarifies.'

Prevalence was discussed but the reviewer felt this was not written from a patient's perspective. Coverage of the causes of infertility was considered inadequate and the information on treatment options was not felt to be clearly written. Uncertainties and knowledge gaps were not covered, for example the lack of evidence for the effectiveness of cold water therapy. The booklet was considered strong on its coverage of investigations, although the reviewer felt that it contained too much information about superfluous tests. The section on 'coming to terms' was considered 'not very helpful'.

Much of the information was felt to be out of date and some was inaccurate, for example, the pregnancy rates given were too high, and limitations of drug treatments were not discussed. The reviewer felt that the treatment choices were not well laid out and not clearly related to the problem and there was too much information on gonadotrophin drugs produced by the sponsors.

So you want to have a baby?: Serono Laboratories

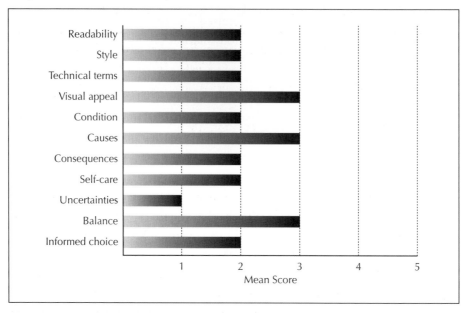

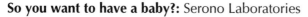

Infertility: Women's Health

Overall ratings: Patients   8.8 (range 7–10) rank 1=
                    Specialist   5.0 rank 2

Publication date: 1990

Address: Women's Health, 52 Featherstone Street, London EC1Y 8RT.

Description

This is an eight-page black and white leaflet illustrated with one cartoon and three anatomical diagrams. Sections include: who is affected?; how is it defined?; how is it experienced?; counselling; what can go wrong?; protecting your fertility; causes in women; attending a clinic; tests; treatments; complementary therapy; male infertility; treatment for men; other causes; conclusion; glossary; further information.

Patients' views

This leaflet was rated highly by all four women, although several of them said that their first impression of it was that it would be hard going and they might not have bothered to pick it up to read if they had come across it by chance.

The leaflet was generally judged to be informative, and its coverage of the psychological and social impact of reduced fertility was particularly appreciated. A comment from one woman who suggested that there was not enough detail about several treatment options triggered a discussion about the fine balance between including too much information in a leaflet and not enough. The reading list, glossary and list of self-help groups were thought to be helpful.

The leaflet was considered easy to read and friendly.

Academic specialist's views

This leaflet, which achieved reasonably good ratings for most features, was appreciated by the reviewer despite its low budget approach and limited graphics: 'Brief, to the point, well laid out, although low budget production'. It was felt to provide clear information about the condition, was well presented and readable. The reviewer felt it would serve as a good introduction to the topic, with a good glossary and helpful list of sources of further information. However, the information about risks and benefits of treatment options was felt to be brief and too superficial in some important areas. For example, the information on IVF was considered poor, with no coverage of risks. The lack of detail was felt to inhibit its usefulness in promoting informed choice.

Infertility: Women's Health

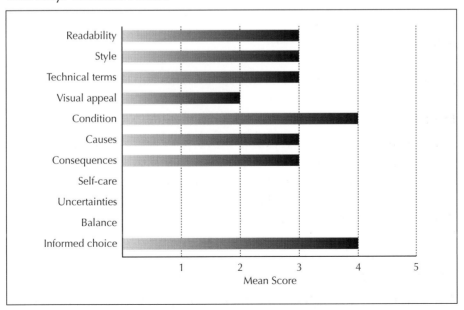

Female Infertility, Male Infertility: PPP Healthcare Health Information Line Factsheets

Overall ratings: Patients   4.5 (range 4–5) rank 5
                      Specialist   4.0 rank 3

Publication date: No date on factsheets.

Address: PPP Healthcare Ltd, PPP House, Vale Road, Tunbridge Wells, Kent TN1 1BJ.

Description

These five-page factsheets are simply produced, black on white, with no illustrations. Both cover the following issues: what is female/male infertility?; why does it occur?; how does it occur?; what are the tests?; what is the treatment?; where can I get further information?; information sources.

Patients' views

Although the mere existence of a factsheet about male infertility was appreciated, these two leaflets were spoken of disparagingly. They were considered too brief to be of use as anything but the most basic introduction, and the women disputed the accuracy of some of the information presented because it conflicted with other information they had read.

The tone of the sheets was considered patronising, and there was a view that they tended to dismiss the problem. Although they were deemed inadequate sources of information for people actually having infertility problems, a suggestion that they might be useful for their family, friends or employers met with general agreement.

The women were wary of the motives of PPP Healthcare in producing these materials.

Academic specialist's views

The reviewer liked the style, layout and brevity of these factsheets and the clarity of the introduction and description of the causes of infertility, but was critical of some of the content. In particular the discussion of tests and treatment options was considered too brief to be useful and some of it was inaccurate or out of date. 'Too much prominence given to BBT (now considered unhelpful) and PCT (poor repeatability and prognostic value)'. The information on treatments for male infertility was 'succinct and inaccurate'.

In general these leaflets were felt to contain too little information to promote informed choice: 'Too little on treatment options including implications and side-effects'.

Female infertility, male infertility: PPP Healthcare

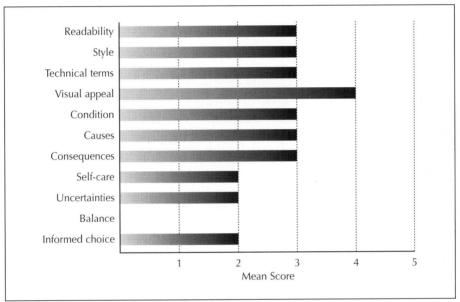

Information pack, including: *NURTURE booklet, patient information document and You could help make a miracle leaflet:* Nottingham University Research and Treatment Unit in Reproduction (NURTURE)

Overall ratings: Patients   8.3 (range 7–9) rank 3
                Specialist   6.0 rank 1

Publication date: July 1996

Address: Nottingham University Research and Treatment Unit
                        in Reproduction, Department of Obstetrics and
                        Gynaecology, Floor B, East Block, University Hospital,
                        Queen's Medical Centre, Nottingham NG7 2UH.

Description

This pack of information contains a glossy 20-page brochure describing the
NURTURE unit, a newsletter, a colour leaflet on egg donation, You could help
make a miracle, a separate leaflet outlining advances in managing male factor
infertility, a single sheet giving information about treatment results in the
period 1 April 1994 to 31 March 1995, the fees schedule from 1 December
1996 and a patient information document covering IVF and ICSI treatments.

The brochure provides background information about sub-fertility and sub-
fertility management and gives information about NURTURE's patient
services. The patient information document is intended as a guide to the assisted
conception treatment cycle to be read in conjunction with individualised
treatment protocols which are sent to patients on a cycle by cycle basis. The *You
could help make a miracle* leaflet is aimed at recruiting donors for the egg
donation programme. Each of the documents was written by a clinical expert
and circulated widely amongst all grades of Unit staff for their comments
before finalising. Patients' comments on earlier versions were taken into
account when revising the brochure and the patient information leaflet.
None of the leaflets has been formally evaluated.

Patients' views

This pack differed in focus from the other materials considered. The women
felt that the whole package was a sales brochure intended for people who were
going to pay for private IVF treatment and deciding where to go to have it.
For someone who was going to have IVF, the patient information leaflet was
thought to provide useful (specific) information about the processes they
would go through.

The price list generated interest and a couple of women read the newsletter.
Opinions differed about the appropriateness of including a leaflet about egg
donation in the pack.

The women's ratings reported above were for the patient information leaflet
alone, ignoring the glossy brochure, newsletter and price list.

Academic specialist's views

The reviewer appreciated the clarity of style and content of these materials, but noted the fact that there was a strong emphasis on advertising the NURTURE clinic. The professional presentation and friendly style was commended: 'Very well laid out. Top of the range for presentation'.

The patient information leaflet was not intended to present information about all treatment options, since it was aimed only at couples seeking IVF treatment. AIH and tubal surgery were mentioned, but only briefly. The reviewer felt that insufficient attention was given to the risks of IVF and the causes of infertility. This leaflet was not considered helpful as a general guide to treatment choices for infertility.

NURTURE: Nottingham University

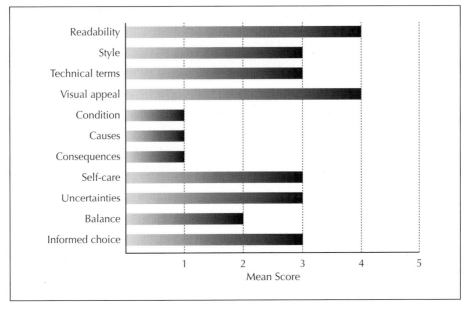

Chapter 17

Menorrhagia

Focus group

The focus group comprised five women aged between 45 and 52 years. All had had children and three currently lived with a partner. The women varied greatly in the length of time for which they had suffered from menorrhagia. Two women had had the problem for 20 years or more (one since the age of 13, the other since the birth of her second child); one for eight years; and two for less than two years.

One woman also mentioned suffering from bad anaemia and depression, and another had migraines. None of the women were members of self-help groups. One woman had worked previously at a Well Woman's Centre and had obtained some information from there.

Academic specialists

Reviewers included a university research lecturer in gynaecological medicine, a professor of gynaecology, and a general practitioner with a special interest in women's health.

The materials

Abnormal Vaginal Bleeding: Women's Health Concern (WHC)
Heavy Periods: Jessop Hospital, Sheffield
Heavy Periods: Royal College of Obstetricians and Gynaecologists (RCOG)
Abnormal Uterine Bleeding: Krames Communications
Coping with Heavy Bleeding: Women's Health

Rankings

	Patients	Specialists
1	RCOG	RCOG
2	Jessop	Krames
3	Women's Health	Jessop
4	WHC	Women's Health (3=)
5	Krames	WHC

Summary of reviews

All the materials reviewed were leaflets or booklets. The booklet produced by the Royal College of Obstetricians and Gynaecologists was the most popular, with both groups ranking it highest, although the specialists felt it was too biased towards surgery. The leaflet produced by the Jessop Hospital was seen as containing much useful information, although its presentation was not very polished. Patients were very divided in their opinions on the Krames booklet, some of them taking a violent dislike to the illustrations. The specialists were much more enthusiastic about this booklet, although they felt some of the information was out of date. The specialists were more critical of the content of the Women's Health leaflet and the one produced by Women's Health Concern.

Specialists considered that only the RCOG booklet and the one from Jessop Hospital attempted to provide information to inform choices and neither of these did it very well. Since this is a condition for which there is a range of options, on which patients' preferences may be expected to differ, it was felt particularly disappointing that these materials failed to provide real support for informed decision-making.

Abnormal Vaginal Bleeding: Women's Health Concern, sponsored by Parke-Davis Research Laboratories

---

Overall ratings: Patients   5.8 (range 5–8) rank 4 (out of 5)

                           Specialists   4.0 (range 1–7) rank 5

Publication date: 1991

Address: Women's Health Concern Ltd, PO Box 1629, London W8 6AU.

Description

This fold-out leaflet was written by two gynaecologists (including one of the specialist reviewers). It contains no illustrations. The contents cover classification, diagnosis, menstrual blood loss measurement, medical and surgical treatments.

Patients' views

Discussion of this leaflet was generally negative. The language and tone used were the focus of most of the criticism. The leaflet was perceived as 'too clinical', 'too technical', 'impersonal' and 'condescending'. The use of the word 'abnormal' in the title and text was particularly disliked, and the leaflet was felt to be unduly negative. The group generally agreed with the woman who said: 'If I'd only had this leaflet, I'd have been very worried ... If I'd only had this one I think it would have made me feel almost upset'.

The organisation of material was described as 'logical', but the women made several comments suggesting that it reflected a (male) medical rather than a woman's perspective. One woman reported having been surprised that it was produced by Women's Health Concern – she had assumed it was written by 'a bunch of highfalutin' consultants'. The statement 'Hysterectomy is the ultimate solution for abnormal bleeding' was singled out for criticism and the leaflet was felt to lack practical ideas and suggestions for self-help.

On the positive side, the small size of the leaflet and the provision of the telephone number of a counselling service were appreciated.

Academic specialists' views

The two specialists not involved in its production were unenthusiastic about this leaflet. One said: 'Very poor readability factor – I found it rather tough going and I think I'd be more frightened by the end of it.' Another felt it contained too much technical jargon and was biased. 'Overemphasises prostaglandins and treatment with Ponstan which reduces bleeding by inadequate amount (25 per cent). Clearly, Parke-Davis sponsorship has influenced the recommendations.' It was considered cold and patronising in tone.

Two reviewers criticised the leaflet for not including enough information to help a woman judge whether her bleeding is excessive and for failing to provide statistics to back up the claim that menorrhagia is a common problem. They felt it did not provide clear definitions of technical terms, failed to discuss self-care and omitted information about several treatments including the option of no treatment. Specialist reviewers pointed out that it did not discuss the relative effects of the different treatments or the risks.

Abnormal vaginal bleeding: Women's Health Concern

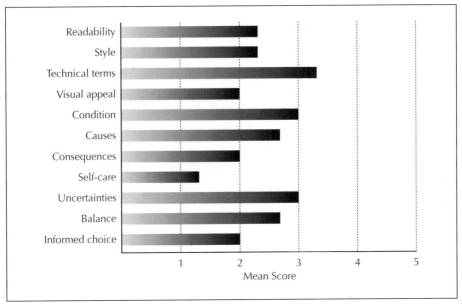

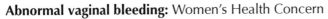

Heavy Periods: Jessop Hospital for Women, Sheffield

Overall ratings: Patients   7.8 (range 6–9) rank 2
                      Specialists   6.0 (range 5–7) rank 3=

Publication date: No date on leaflet.

Address: Jessop Hospital for Women, Leavygreave Road,
                      Sheffield S3 7RD.

Description

This is a simple eight-page A5 leaflet without illustrations, photocopied and folded, not stapled. Sections include: bleeding patterns; seeing your GP; common causes of bleeding; seeing your doctor; drug treatment available from GPs; seeing a gynaecologist; operations for heavy bleeding; helping yourself; alternative therapies; further reading.

Patients' views

This leaflet was generally liked and contained information about causes and treatment options which some of the women had not come across before. The content areas singled out for positive comment included the list of possible causes of heavy periods, the section entitled 'Helping yourself' and the suggestions for dealing with stress. The group particularly appreciated the way the leaflet explicitly recognised that heavy periods can be disruptive and debilitating.

The clear title and simple, straightforward, reassuring and 'friendly' language were all appreciated. The women got the impression that it was written by 'somebody who knows what they're talking about' and who actually 'wants women to know'.

On the negative side, the presentation of the leaflet was considered a bit drab and 'amateurish'. This had caused initial opinions of the leaflet to be less favourable than those formed after reading it.

Academic specialists' views

The content of this cheaply produced leaflet was appreciated more than its visual appeal. It was considered good on 'common causes of bleeding', discussion of anaemia and lifestyle effects, but lacked statistics to put this in context. It was criticised for failing to define terms: 'Quite a lot of big words, e.g. "laparoscopically assisted vaginal hysterectomy ..." They've forgotten normal people don't know what this is.'

Uncertainties and knowledge gaps were felt to be not well covered, and reviewers pointed out that it lacked detail on prognosis, the pros and cons of the different treatment options and the risks.

Heavy periods: Jessop Hospital, Sheffield

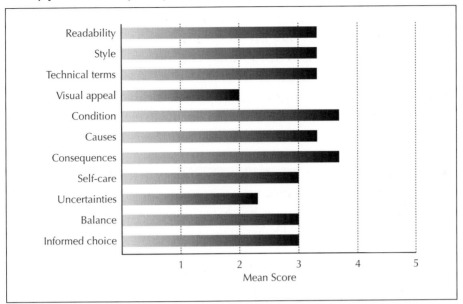

Heavy Periods: Royal College of Obstetricians and Gynaecologists

Overall ratings: Patients   8.6 (range 8–10) rank 1
                        Specialists   7.3 (range 7–8) rank 1

Publication date: 1994

Address: Royal College of Obstetricians and Gynaecologists,
                        27 Sussex Place, Regent's Park, London NW1 4RG.

Description

A 12-page two-colour booklet which contains three illustrations (anatomical diagrams illustrating fibroids and polyps, hysterectomy and endometrial resection). Sections cover: is it a common problem?; do not feel embarrassed; how do I know if my periods are heavy?; what causes my periods to be heavy?; what should I do if my periods are heavy (including drug treatment)?; what will the gynaecologist suggest (diagnostic tests)?; what treatment is best for you (hysterectomy, endometrial resection, myomectomy)?; what to do if you feel you are not being taken seriously?; meaning of medical terms used.

Patients' views

All the women rated this booklet highly and found much to praise about its content and presentation. They felt it was suitable for women of all ages with heavy periods, and suggested that it would help women realise that they did not need to just put up with the problem of heavy periods and encourage them to discuss the problem and the different treatment options with their doctors. The section on 'What to do if you feel you are not being taken seriously' was particularly liked.

When asked whether they thought the risks of the different treatment options had been adequately covered, the women responded that although some side-effects were mentioned, the risks had been 'glossed over'. Overall, however, they thought the leaflet would help people to make treatment choices.

The modern cover gave the women the impression that the booklet was up to date, and the clear language and glossary made it easy to read. The women had confidence in the booklet and felt that it gave them confidence.

Academic specialists' views

The specialists liked this booklet – 'good, comprehensive and well illustrated', 'friendly style, reassuring to patient' – although they felt it placed undue emphasis on surgical procedures and glossed over gaps in the research evidence. It was commended for its description of the effects of the problem on a woman's daily life and for the discussion of the causes and consequences of the problem. It received high marks for its definitions of technical terms and its visual appeal, but was criticised for failing to cover self-help options, for scanty information on the efficacy of drug treatments and lack of clear information on the risks and side-effects of surgery.

Reviewers felt the information was not sufficient to support informed treatment choice, since it was biased towards surgery and encouraged an underestimation of the risks. It was also criticised for being out of date and for recommending ineffective treatments.

Heavy periods: Royal College of Obstetricians and Gynaecologists

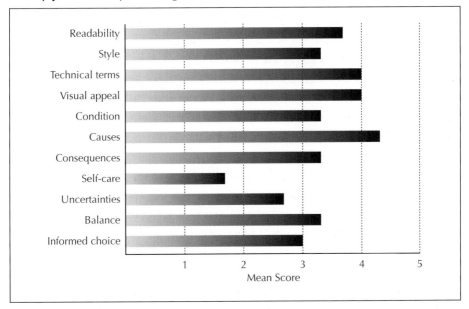

Abnormal Uterine Bleeding: Krames Communications

Overall ratings:	Patients	5.2 (range 1–8) rank 5
	Specialists	7.0 (range 6–7) rank 2

Publication date:	1992

Address:	Krames Communications, 1100 Grundy Lane, San Bruno, California 94066-3030, USA.

Description

This 16-page booklet is amply illustrated in full colour. Sections include: when bleeding disrupts your life; getting your bleeding under control; common questions; normal menstrual bleeding; what is normal menstruation?; hormones control menstrual cycles; your reproductive organs; your evaluation; medical history; pelvic exam; bleeding record; possible causes of abnormal uterine bleeding; diagnostic tests; hormonal imbalances; causes of hormonal imbalances; dysfunctional uterine bleeding; treating a hormonal imbalance; is hormone therapy right for you?; controlled bleeding; uterine growths; your surgical options; your bleeding record.

Patients' views

Discussion of this booklet focused heavily on the illustrations, which were disliked by most of the women – some women reacted so negatively to them that they were put off reading the booklet. The illustrations would also have prevented some of the women from showing the booklet to their partners or family. Several women agreed that this booklet would not have helped them to make informed treatment choices because (apart from the fact that non-hormonal drugs were not mentioned) the pictures were so frighteningly gory that they would have put them off having the interventions that were illustrated.

Features of the booklet that were liked included the chart at the back that would help women ascertain whether or not their periods were heavy, the inclusion of women of different races and ages in the illustrations, and the emphasis in the text on women 'taking control' of the problem. Interestingly, the women felt that the illustrations tended to contradict the positive verbal messages about taking control because they appeared to portray the women as indecisive victims, and because the doctors were always depicted above the patients, and talking to/at them rather than listening. The use of the term 'abnormal' was again felt to be inappropriate.

Subject specialists' views

The specialists were much more enthusiastic about this US booklet than the patients. 'Wow! Real Hollywood stuff. I loved its visual impact – made you feel real women had the problem. I liked the idea of the patient *taking control*. Very friendly, informative and encouraging women to ask questions.' However, it was criticised for its description of the problem, for containing out-of-date information on the causes of dysfunctional bleeding and too much emphasis on hormonal imbalance. Many treatments commonly used in Britain were omitted, e.g. NSAIDs, tranexamic acid, Mirena coil, danazol.

The booklet was commended for promoting a positive view but reviewers pointed out that it contained little information about self-help strategies. There was no discussion about uncertainties: 'I don't think Americans believe in uncertainty ...' All three specialists felt the booklet was biased in favour of surgery and the information on medical treatments was out of date and not evidence-based.

Abnormal uterine bleeding: Krames Communications

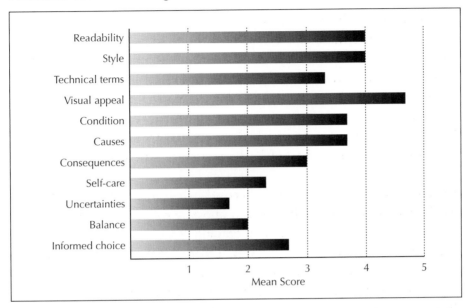

Coping with Heavy Bleeding: Women's Health

Overall ratings: Patients   7.6 (range 6–9) rank 3
    Specialists   6.0 (range 4–8) rank 3=

Publication date: 1995

Address: Women's Health, 52 Featherstone Street, London EC1Y 8RT.

Description

This leaflet consists of eight A4 sheets stapled together, printed in black and white with four wood-cut illustrations. Sections include: what is heavy bleeding?; clots; what causes heavy bleeding?; how is heavy bleeding affecting me?; sanitary protection; medical response to heavy bleeding – investigations; when a cause is found; fibroids; when no cause is found; tablets; treatment of anaemia; D&C; endometrial aspiration; TCRE; laser ablation; hysterectomy; bioflavonoids; holistic remedies – herbalism, homeopathy, aromatherapy, acupuncture and Chinese herbal medicine; further resources.

Patients' views

The leaflet was generally perceived to be informative and the emphasis on practical self-help measures was appreciated. The women liked the fact that other women with experience of the problem had informed the content of the leaflet: they felt the authors really 'knew' the kinds of difficulties they had to contend with and made positive suggestions for 'coping'.

The inclusion of information about alternative therapies was generally appreciated, although some found the section a little confusing, and one woman observed that the leaflet appeared to imply that either medical treatments or holistic ones could be used, whereas in fact both could be employed at the same time. The woman who gave this leaflet the lowest rating said that, although it presented lots of options, 'It mentions so much about the side-effects of all of them, I really thought "Ugh, nothing's going to be very good".'

Four of the five women liked the tone of the leaflet, which they described as 'friendly', 'womanly' and positive. The other woman did appreciate the 'woman to woman' approach, and agreed that the authors understood what women with heavy periods went through, but felt that the leaflet didn't seem to relate to how she saw herself.

Academic specialists' views

This leaflet was praised for containing a great deal of information, including a 'good first general section with stories of real women with heavy periods to give you an idea of what misery some women put up with'. It was criticised because much of the treatment information was not evidence-based. The style and tone were considered friendly and unpatronising, but some of the language was felt to be too complex. One reviewer felt the leaflet lacked visual appeal; 'solid prose with gloomy wood-cuts'. Some medical terms were not explained, but the leaflet was commended for providing details women want to know, e.g. about how long you bleed after a D&C.

The discussion of diagnostic tests was felt to be confused with an overemphasis on D&C and too little on hysteroscopy or scans. The information on medical treatments and complementary therapies was considered misleading and inaccurate, with no discussion of the relative efficacy of these treatments. Specialists felt this limited the usefulness of this leaflet in promoting shared decision-making.

Coping with heavy bleeding: Women's Health

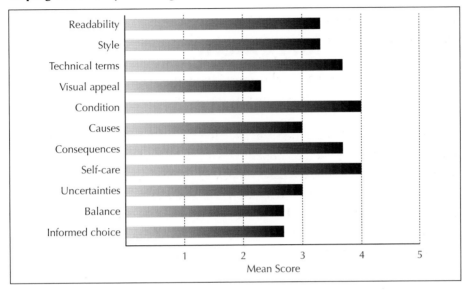

Chapter 18

Prostate enlargement

Focus group

The focus group comprised nine men aged between 54 and 75 (four men were over 70 years old and two under 60). They had all experienced prostate related problems for between three and twenty years, but none of them, as far as they were aware, had prostatitis or prostate cancer.

The men had undergone a range of diagnostic tests between them. Three had had surgery for their prostate problems, and two had received drug treatment only. Four of the men had not received any treatment interventions.

Five of the men were members of the Prostate Help Association, and three had used contacts from current or previous employment positions (as a dental surgeon, pharmaceutical retailer and health service quantity surveyor) as sources of information. The focus group members recognised that they were a self-selected group of men who were particularly interested in their health problems and perhaps more able and willing than most to access information.

Academic specialists

The subject specialists included a professor of surgery, a consultant urologist, and a professor of epidemiology.

The materials

Half of All Men over 50 Have This Complaint: Invicta Pharmaceuticals
Surgery on the Prostate: The Royal College of Surgeons of England (RCS)
What Every Man Should Know about Prostate Problems: Scriptographic Publications
Benign Prostatic Enlargement: PatientWise
What You Really Need to Know about Enlarged Prostate: Videos for Patients Prostate Problems/Prostatectomy: College of Health

Rankings

	Patients	Specialists
1	RCS	RCS
2	Scriptographic	College of Health
3	Videos for Patients	Scriptographic
4	PatientWise	Videos for Patients (3=)
5	Invicta	PatientWise
6	College of Health	Invicta

Summary of reviews

Materials reviewed included three booklets, a factsheet, a video and a telephone helpline. The Royal College of Surgeons booklet was given the highest ratings by both patients and specialists, both groups finding it helpful, comprehensive and attractive. Patients were also enthusiastic about the Scriptographic booklet, but specialists were a little more critical. Specialists gave higher rankings to the helpline than the patients, who found it quite difficult to hear the tape. The Invicta leaflet was not much liked, being seen simply as an 'awareness raiser' and containing little useful information. Views on the video and the PatientWise factsheet were mixed, the latter attracting a particularly wide range of scores.

The Royal College of Surgeons booklet was commended for providing detailed information about surgical options, but alternatives to surgery were only briefly discussed. The Scriptographic booklet covered most of the options, but specialists felt it did not include enough information about outcome probabilities to be really useful in promoting informed choice. The tone of the video and the helpline tapes were criticised for failing to encourage patients to express their preferences and make choices, and the PatientWise factsheet and the Invicta leaflet were considered too basic and incomplete to promote shared decision-making.

Half of All Men over 50 Have This Complaint: Invicta
Pharmaceuticals (Pfizer Ltd)

Overall ratings:	Patients	5.4 (range 3–7) rank 5 (out of 6)
	Specialists	4.7 (range 4–6) rank 6

Publication date: No date on leaflet.

Address: Pfizer Ltd, Sandwich, Kent CT13 9NJ.

Description

This is a six-page booklet with four illustrations, including diagrams of the urinary system. Sections are included on: what controls urine flow in men?; why do many men develop bladder problems?; benign prostatic hypertrophy; how could BPH affect you?; can an enlarged prostate be treated?; what should you do?

The producers of this leaflet gave the following response to our request for further information: 'This is an old leaflet which we no longer use. We have no stocks of the leaflet left, and there are no plans to update or reprint it. It seems inappropriate, therefore, to complete the questionnaire you sent.'

Patients' views

Members of the focus group recognised that this was an 'introductory leaflet' that 'anybody' could pick up. Most of the group found the title and front cover eye-catching and thought people would be encouraged to pick the leaflet up because it appeared to be relevant to them. One of the most positive comments about this leaflet was that it tended to be reassuring, particularly because it conveyed the message to men with symptoms of prostate problems that they were not alone. The level of detail provided about treatments, however, was felt to be inadequate (although not necessarily for a truly introductory leaflet). As one man commented, 'It doesn't give even enough information to base the beginnings of a decision on'.

Members of the focus group had recognised that the leaflet came from a commercial source, but while some said this would make them read the leaflet in the same way as they would read an advertisement, at least one person had assumed that the pharmaceutical company had sponsored the production of a medical booklet.

The text of the leaflet was thought to be unattractively laid out and rather 'heavy' in places.

Academic specialists' views

This was seen as an introductory leaflet designed to get men to consult their doctors about this problem, but providing little information on treatment options. Drugs and surgery are mentioned, but specialists felt it was insufficiently detailed. One reviewer said of this leaflet: 'It is simply meant to act as an awareness raiser and might be very useful in a GP's surgery, although it is only half way through the booklet that one realises what the booklet is about. Thus for its purpose this might be quite good.'

It scored reasonably high marks for style and readability, but low for self-care, coverage of medical uncertainties and promoting informed choice. One reviewer considered the illustrations confusing, 'I can't understand them.'

Half of all men over 50 have this complaint: Invicta Pharmaceuticals

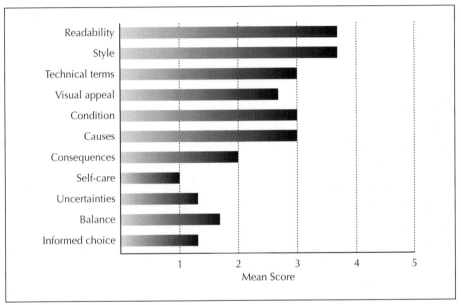

Surgery on the Prostate: The Royal College of Surgeons of England

| Overall ratings: | Patients | 9.0 (range 8–10) rank 1 |
| | Specialists | 8.0 (range 8) rank 1 |

Publication date: 1994

Address: The Surgical Audit Unit, The Royal College of Surgeons of England, 35/43 Lincoln's Inn Fields, London WC2A 3PN.

Description

This 40-page full-colour A5 booklet is amply illustrated with drawings and diagrams. Sections include: how you can best use this booklet; your prostate and what can go wrong; making decisions: the outpatient clinic meeting; about the operation; about the hospital stay; the operation; in the weeks following the operation; if I have any questions or comments.

The booklet, which was designed to be used by all potential prostatectomy patients prior to their first outpatient visit, aims to provide detailed information on the condition, on decision-making and on the hospital stay. The content draws on literature reviews and on material collected in the RCS National Prostatectomy Audit, including comments from patients about their information needs. It has been evaluated by means of a questionnaire survey to patients and there are plans to revise it.

Patients' views

This booklet was highly rated by everyone in the focus group because it was perceived to be comprehensive (it gave at least one person information that he hadn't had before), simply written, and honest about the shortcomings and complications of treatment. The men felt that this booklet would help them to identify and ask relevant questions.

The men had noticed that the booklet was produced by the Royal College of Surgeons, and while this generally added to its credibility, an emphasis on surgery and relative lack of information about medical treatments was detected (although as one man pointed out, the leaflet was called *Surgery on the Prostate* and not *Treatment of the Prostate*). It was also suggested that the booklet did not cover diagnostic tests well, and did not mention some of the newer surgical techniques.

Academic specialists' views

Two of the three specialist reviewers were involved in the production of this booklet. All were enthusiastic about the booklet which was described as well presented, comprehensive and sympathetic. The visual appeal was considered excellent, with good layout and diagrams. It scored high marks across the board except for self-care which was 'hardly mentioned'.

Specialists noted that the booklet contained comprehensive information about diagnostic procedures and treatment options including TURP, open prostatectomy, bladder neck incision, laser and microwave surgery, drugs and watchful waiting. However, while surgical treatments were covered in detail, alternatives to surgery (e.g. drugs) were only briefly discussed.

Surgery on the prostate: The Royal College of Surgeons of England

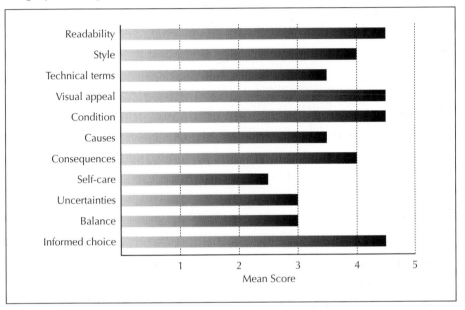

Mean Score

What Every Man Should Know about Prostate Problems:
Scriptographic Publications Ltd

Overall ratings:	Patients	8.5 (range 7–9) rank 2
	Specialists	6.0 (range 6) rank 3=

Publication date: 1996

Address: Scriptographic Publications Ltd, Channing House, Butts Road, Alton, Hants, GU34 1ND.

Description

This is a 16-page A5 booklet in two colours amply illustrated with line drawings and diagrams. Sections cover: what is the prostate?; why is it important to know about the prostate?; benign prostatic hyperplasia; prostatitis; prostate cancer; how prostate problems are diagnosed; types of prostate surgery; prostate disease treatment and your sex life; take steps to prevent prostate problems; sources of help and information; most prostate problems can be treated.

The booklet is intended for all men concerned about their health, to be distributed in primary and secondary care. It aims to provide an overview of the causes, symptoms and treatment of the major types of prostate problems. It is produced by a company which specialises in patient information, all of whose booklets are subject to periodic review. The content draws on market research about patients' information needs, published research articles and specialist knowledge of clinical experts. Patients were not directly involved in the production of the booklet.

Patients' views

This booklet was highly rated by everyone in the focus group primarily because of its clarity and attractive presentation. All the men liked the short blocks of text and related diagrams. The inclusion of information about prevention was also liked.

Although briefer than the Royal College of Surgeons' booklet, this leaflet was also described as 'comprehensive'. One man suggested that this leaflet was like the *Concise Oxford Dictionary* in relation to the Royal College of Surgeons' booklet which was like the *Full Oxford Dictionary*. The men thought this leaflet would be useful for men who had been referred to a specialist by their general practitioner. They thought it would help prepare people to see the consultant, ask questions, and understand what they were told.

The men had noticed that the leaflet was American, and felt that there were some discrepancies between what the leaflet recommended and what was available to them in practice on the NHS.

Academic specialists' views

The specialists liked the clear, simple style of this booklet and the helpful diagrams. They pointed out that there was little coverage of the causes of the conditions although most treatment options were mentioned, and there was almost no information on prognostic factors and outcome probabilities. The tone was felt to be somewhat didactic and uncertainties were not really discussed. The information was considered insufficient to promote shared decision-making.

What every man should know about prostate problems: Scriptographic
Publications

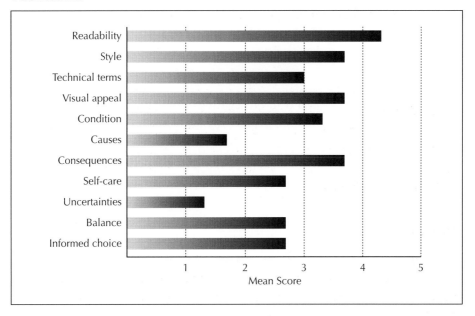

Benign Prostatic Enlargement: Patient Wise, Wiley

Overall ratings: Patients   6.6 (range 2–7) rank 4
                      Specialists   5.3 (range 2–8) rank 5

Publication date: 1995

Address: PatientWise, John Wiley & Sons Ltd, 1 Oldlands Way,
                     Bognor Regis, West Sussex, PO22 9SA.

Description

This factsheet is part of a set covering many common conditions designed to
be given to patients by their GPs or hospital consultants. The latest version is
designed to be accessed via 'Healthpoint' outlets and in public libraries. It can
be photocopied from a loose-leaf volume or printed out from a software version.

The sheet has been updated since it was reviewed, the new version became
available in March 1997. The format complies with Hellman's 'defined

questions'. All three editors of PatientWise (a physician, a GP and a lay editor) reviewed the leaflet and its readability level was assessed using the Gunning Fog Index. An evaluation of the PatientWise information system was published in the *Journal of the Royal Society of Medicine* (vol 89, Oct 1996, pp. 557–60).

Patients' views

This leaflet attracted a good deal of negative comment from the focus group participants, one of whom 'couldn't think of anything good to say about it'. It was felt to be 'dreadfully' presented, with heavy blocks of text, a lot of technical terminology and a very alarmist tone. The men thought that unless the leaflet was given to them by a health professional before or during a consultation, they would be unlikely to pick it up or read it.

Although the purpose and intended audience of the leaflet was not clear, some men surmised that it was perhaps meant to be given to people who were waiting to see a consultant. One suggested that it gave a good description of the treatment which one could receive in the hospital 'but purely just that'.

On the positive side, one man had appreciated the explanation of why the degree of enlargement of the prostate did not relate directly to the amount of difficulty experienced in passing urine.

Academic specialists' views

The factsheet was commended for giving a basic introduction to the subject, but specialists felt it lacked sufficient detail to promote shared decision-making. It provided no information about the causes of the condition and several treatment options were omitted, including self-help, alpha blockers, interstitial treatments, focused ultrasound and open prostatectomy.

One reviewer pointed to inaccuracies in the text: 'The natural history is inaccurate and overly gloomy.' The factsheet was criticised for its dense, small text and its lack of pictures.

Benign prostatic enlargement: Patient Wise

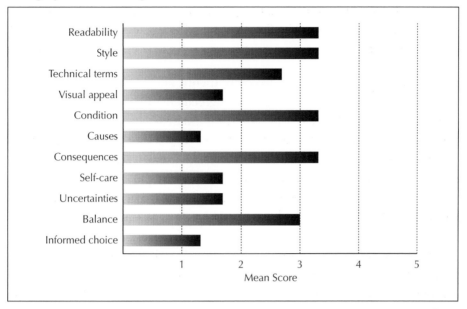

What You Really Need to Know about Enlarged Prostate: Videos for
Patients, Video Arts Productions Ltd

Overall ratings: Patients   8.1 (range 6–9) rank 3
                      Specialists   6.0 (range 4–8) rank 3=

Publication date: 1994

Address: Video Arts Ltd, 18 Denbigh Close, London W11 2QH.

Description

This video was written and produced by Dr Rob Buckman and John Cleese.
The aim is to give patients (and their carers) a full understanding of their
medical condition in an easy to understand way (avoiding medical jargon).
Contents include: what is enlargement of the prostate all about? what is the
prostate and what does it do? what problems does an enlarged prostate cause?
what is likely to happen next? how is the diagnosis made? how is enlargement
of the prostate treated? medications that can help; the TURP surgical procedure;
other surgical procedures; where can I get more information and help?

Available via GPs, the series of videos is currently being piloted in Bromley Health Authority, with reviews and feedback from GPs and patients.

Patients' views

The men generally rated the video quite highly, and praised it for being clear and comprehensive. There was general agreement though, that it was over-optimistic about treatments and lacked information about the side-effects of drugs and the risks of surgery.

There were mixed views about the suitability of the presenter. John Cleese is associated with humour, and while some men were disappointed that the video was presented in such a serious way and felt it would have benefited from an injection of humour, others felt that for such a serious topic, a man so associated with humour was not appropriate. The video was criticised for being condescending, partly because it was 'pedestrian' and 'repetitive'.

Academic specialists' views

The video included very detailed information on TURP, although one reviewer considered the information about retrograde ejaculation inaccurate. Information about drugs and new surgical treatments was felt to be very limited and it was criticised for containing little information on self-help. Specialists felt it could have benefited from more use of graphics.

Specialists differed in their response to this video, with one describing it as 'very well presented, friendly and reassuring', while another described it as 'very slow, patronising, no information about choices'. The tone was considered fairly didactic, assuming that decisions would be taken by the doctor. In general it was felt to present a fairly rosy view of surgery.

What you really need to know about enlarged prostate: Videos for Patients

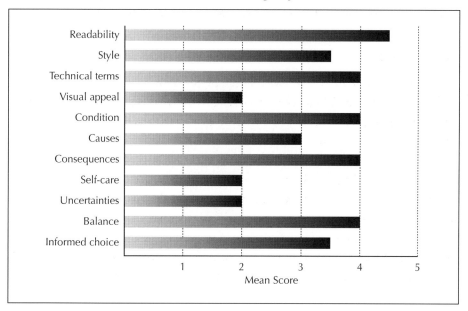

Prostate Problems/Prostatectomy: College of Health

Overall ratings:	Patients	5.3 (range 3–7) rank 6
	Specialists	6.3 (range 6–7) rank 2

Publication date: 1996

Address: College of Health, St Margaret's House, 21 Old Ford Road, London E2 9PL.

Description

This audiotape can be accessed by dialling a helpline number. It describes the causes of BPH; symptoms; diagnosis; treatment options; undergoing surgery; and where to go for more information and self-help groups.

It was last revised October 1996 and the next revision is planned for May 1997.

Patients' views

Only four participants listened to this helpline, and they had found it hard to understand because of the 'terribly poor' quality of the tape. One person had rung five or six times and even tried to record it in an attempt to be able to hear what was being said. There was also a view that the use of a female commentator to talk about prostate problems was 'most unsuitable'.

Although the presentation was very poor, the few people who had listened to the tape made broadly favourable comments about its contents, describing it as 'quite comprehensive', 'quite good' and 'all right as a quickie'. One person was particularly pleased that the tape, in contrast to the other materials, had mentioned microwave treatment as being successful. This had coincided with his own views ('I'm quite optimistic about microwave treatment'). The mention of post-operative exercises was also favourably commented on.

Academic specialists' views

While the tape included information on TURP, open prostatectomy and drugs, specialists noted that the benefits were assumed and the risks barely covered. The tape concentrates on getting men to recognise symptoms and seek medical help and providing clear, relatively simple, concise information on treatment options. It was commended for its style and comprehensibility and for its clear description of the problem. Some treatments were omitted and specialists felt it was fairly didactic with little emphasis on self-help. It did not score highly on promoting informed choice.

Prostate problems/prostatectomy: College of Health

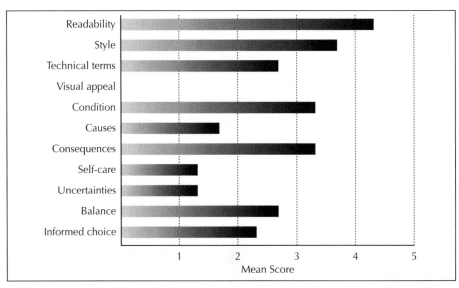

Chapter 19

Stroke

Focus group

The five participants of this focus group included three women and two men, whose ages ranged from late 30s to early 70s. All the participants had been in paid employment before their strokes, two in teaching, one as an air traffic controller, one in customer services and one in the music industry.

The participants had had their strokes between one and 19 years ago. The eldest man had had two strokes. He was the only man who had not spent several weeks in hospital after the stroke, and had found it difficult to access services. All participants had received at least limited help from physiotherapists or occupational therapists, and two had gone through specialist rehabilitation.

Academic specialists

Reviewers included a consultant in neurological disability, a research physiotherapist, and a consultant neurologist, all of whom had a special interest in stroke.

The materials

Stroke – A patient's guide (audiotape): Chest Heart and Stroke Association (CHSA)
Stroke – Questions and answers: Stroke Association
Recovering after a Stroke: Agency for Health Care Policy and Research (AHCPR)
Stroke: South Manchester NHS Trust
Why Me? The experience of stroke (video): Stroke Association

Rankings

	Patients	Specialists
1	South Manchester	AHCPR
2	AHCPR	Stroke Association leaflet
3	CHSA	Stroke Association video
4	Stroke Association video	CHSA
5	Stoke Association leaflet	South Manchester

Summary of reviews

The patients and specialists gave divergent rankings to these materials, which included three booklets or leaflets, a video and an audiotape. Specialists were very critical of the South Manchester leaflet which was liked by patients. Specialists pointed to many omissions and inaccuracies. Specialists were more enthusiastic about the AHCPR booklet, but they felt it was too American to be of direct relevance to the UK. Neither group was enthusiastic about the presentational style of the Stroke Association booklet, although the content was considered quite useful. Views about the CHSA tape varied widely within the groups, with some people liking it much more than others. The Stroke Association video attracted similarly divergent views, and specialists felt it was not really suitable for patients or their carers.

Treatment options for stroke patients include acute stroke treatments, rehabilitation methods and secondary prevention. Specialists considered that none of the materials reviewed facilitated informed choice in all of these areas and, despite the fact that this topic has attracted much research, many of them contained inaccurate and misleading information.

> ### *Stroke – A patient's guide* (audiotape): Chest, Heart and Stroke Association, Scotland

Overall ratings: Patients   8.0 (range 4–10) rank 3
                    Specialists   5.0 (range 4–7) rank 4

Publication date: 1991

Address: Chest, Heart and Stroke Scotland, 65 North Castle Street, Edinburgh EH2 3LT.

Description

This audiotape is designed for people who have had a stroke and their carers, in particular for those who are dysphasic or cannot read for some reason. It is distributed via stroke liaison nurses working in specialist units. It is based on a booklet which includes the same material. Contents include: causes of stroke; prevention of a second stroke; lifestyle advice and self-help; recovery; feelings and emotions; after-care and rehabilitation; where to get further help; long-term outcomes.

Developed with input from consultants and specialist nurses it has not been formally evaluated, but the publishers report that users say it is helpful to have a voice to listen to as this promotes discussion between patients and carers. A revised version has now been produced.

Patients' views

Most focus group participants rated the tape highly. It was perceived to be a useful 'starting point' that addressed the feelings and needs of the person who had had the stroke and their family and didn't ignore important but sensitive topics like sex. The information about what kind of help (including financial support) they might be able to obtain and from where was particularly appreciated.

The tape was thought to be quite short, and several people identified additional information that they would have liked to be included. One person suggested that reports of patients' own experiences would have enhanced the tape. As an accessible introduction, however, it was perceived to be a useful information resource. The woman who rated the tape lowest criticised it for being too general and appearing to be unstructured.

The tone of the tape was generally liked. It was praised for 'speaking to me as a person' and described as 'positive, informative, constructive and reassuring', 'encouraging and honest'.

Academic specialists' views

Specialists had mixed reactions to this tape: 'I liked the tape when I listened to it but could not remember the key points'; 'A very general introduction to stroke – too short to give any detailed advice or arguments'. The general information about stroke and relevant symptoms was considered useful, but it failed to provide specific information on incidence. Reviewers were also divided in their response to the tone of the recording: 'Direct motivational tone. Sympathetic without being patronising'; 'A bit patronising'.

The tape gives a descriptive account of what will happen and does not discuss treatment options. Specialists pointed out that there was no discussion of the use of aspirin or surgery for secondary prevention, of the benefits of organised care and co-ordinated rehabilitation services, or the possibility of thrombolysis. Advice on self-help was considered 'sensible'. The difficulties in estimating the risk of a second stroke were highlighted, but specialists criticised it for failing to include information about other uncertainties or knowledge gaps. The tape was not felt to provide enough information to facilitate informed choice. 'This tape covers a small topic well. If a comprehensive tape for patients after stroke was required a lot more information should be included. For example: 1. Location of treatment – hospital/home/stroke unit. 2. Type of therapy. 3. Post discharge rehabilitation options'.

Stroke – a patient's guide *(audiotape)*: Chest, Heart and Stroke Association

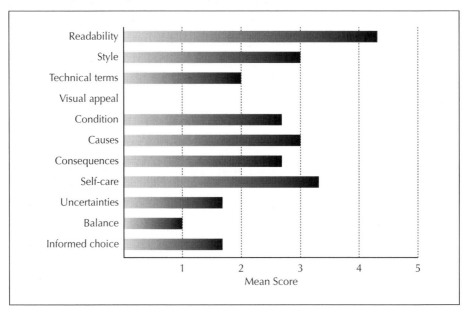

Stroke – Questions and answers: The Stroke Association

Overall ratings:	Patients	6.8 (range 6–10) rank 5
	Specialists	6.3 (range 5–7) rank 2

Publication date: No date on booklet.

Address: The Stroke Association, CHSA House, Whitecross Street, London EC1Y 8JJ.

Description

This is a 16-page A5 booklet without illustrations. Sections include: what is a stroke? what is a transient ischaemic attack? what causes a stroke? is a stroke due to overwork or stress? is the brain affected by a stroke? is the heart affected by a stroke? will recovery occur and how long will it take? what are the risks of a second stroke? do all stroke patients need to go to hospital? how is movement affected? how is speech affected? how is vision affected? what is the medical treatment for a stroke? what is the rehabilitation treatment? should the patient be helped to do everyday tasks or left to 'get on with it'? why does stroke illness tend to make some patients aggressive? what about sexual relationships? what can relatives do to help? where can patients' families get more information about stroke illness? are stroke patients entitled to financial benefits from the state? information about the Stroke Association.

Patients' views

Participants had mixed views about this booklet. On the positive side, it was thought to provide concise and specific answers to the sorts of questions that the participants or their friends had asked. Sources of further information were welcome, as was information about how to help people with stroke. On the negative side, the booklet was felt to be incomplete because it did not mention the possible need for surgery (e.g. after an aneurysm), or counselling. There was also a view that it was not realistic about how movement is affected in some people.

The presentation and tone of the booklet were not considered particularly good. The text was felt to be a 'bit dense' and some people felt that the lack of drawings was a shortcoming. Some people perceived the booklet to be 'distant' and to have 'a coldness about it'. It was criticised for talking about patients not people.

Academic specialists' views

Reviewers did not like the presentation of this booklet: 'Poor presentation, difficult to read'. It was commended for providing direct answers to commonly asked questions and for providing useful information about stroke and its causes and about the incidence and prevalence, but some of the content was considered out of date. 'Does not stress that all strokes are different.' Reference to the heart was considered a bit misleading by one reviewer, who pointed out that many patients confuse heart attack and stroke.

Omissions noted included some causes of stroke (recreational drugs, the Pill, the effect of an ageing population), new diagnostic methods, including computerised scanning, magnetic resonance scanning and the reasons for hospital tests. The booklet was felt to include some good common sense advice on self-care but issues such as driving, employment, and adaptation of accommodation were omitted.

Reviewers pointed out that organised rehabilitation in a stroke unit is one of the few treatment options of proven benefit, but such units are not always available. Coverage of rehabilitation issues in this booklet was described as 'very basic but fair'. The booklet did not include information from recent trials showing benefits of aspirin and thrombolysis and reviewers noted that it did not cover options for post-discharge rehabilitation. Some of the statements were considered inaccurate by reviewers and they felt that uncertainties and knowledge gaps were not well covered.

In general the presentation of this leaflet was not designed to promote informed choice: 'Descriptive account of what happens to someone after stroke. Information not presented in a way to offer patients informed choice. Paragraph on hospital admission prescriptive rather than facilitating active decision-making'.

Stroke – Questions and answers: Stroke Association

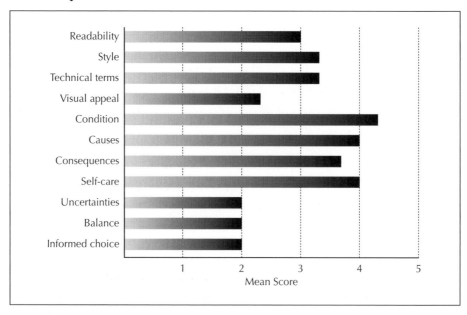

Recovering after a Stroke: Agency for Health Care Policy and Research, US Department of Health and Human Services

Overall ratings: Patients   8.1 (range 5–10) rank 2
                    Specialists   7.3 (range 6–8) rank 1

Publication date: May 1995

Address: Agency for Health Care Policy and Research, Publications Clearinghouse, PO Box 8547, Silver Spring, MD 20907, USA.

Description

This 34-page booklet contains three black and white illustrations. Sections include: what is a stroke? recovering from stroke; how stroke affects people; what happens during acute care; preventing another stroke; deciding about rehabilitation; choosing a rehabilitation programme; what happens during rehabilitation; getting the most out of rehabilitation; discharge planning; sample pages for patient notebook; going home; where to get help; additional resources.

Patients' views

Participants all identified many positive features of this booklet and for some it was the preferred resource, although others felt it was too long. It covered a range of interventions and practical measures that might be useful in different circumstances and sections on 'additional resources', 'where to get help' and 'tips for reducing stress' were particularly liked, as was the consideration given to the whole family.

The straightforward language and clear structure of the booklet contributed to its reader friendliness, and it was praised for 'talking to you as a person'. The overall tone of the booklet was felt to be 'hopeful'.

Academic specialists' views

Reviewers were unanimous in the view that this was the best of the materials on stroke: 'Booklet contains a lot of clear useful information about stroke rehabilitation'; 'Very well written. Easy to read and good explanations'.

They liked the fact that it is clearly laid out with helpful summaries and that it gives the pronunciation of words used by professionals. It was commended for providing good references to other sources of information. But its scope was felt to be limited to post-stroke rehabilitation and little detail was provided on treatments or secondary prevention.

Reviewers felt that much of the information provided was not evidence-based. There was no mention of acute stroke treatments (aspirin and thrombolysis), of the importance of organised care in rehabilitation, or the use of aspirin or carotid surgery for secondary prevention. Uncertainties and knowledge gaps were not referred to and reviewers felt it omitted current research. Reviewers commended it for emphasising the patient's right to choose and participate in decisions, but they felt it did not provide enough information to support them in shared decision-making about treatment options. Reviewers also felt that it was too American to be of direct relevance in the UK.

Recovering after a stroke: Agency for Health Care Policy and Research

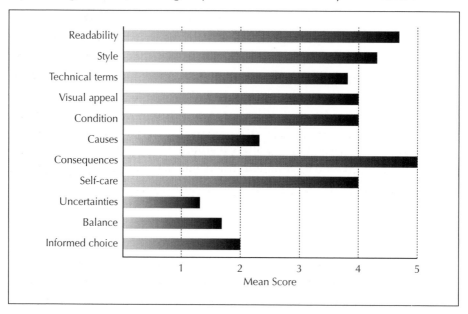

Stroke Patient Information Leaflet: South Manchester University Hospital NHS Trust

Overall ratings: Patients   8.3 (range 8–10) rank 1
                      Specialists   3.3 (range 3–4) rank 5

Publication date: No date on leaflet.

Address: South Manchester University Hospitals NHS Trust,
                      Wythenshawe Hospital, Southmoor Road, Manchester
                      M23 9LT.

Description

This leaflet consist of 12 A4 sheets stapled together with no illustrations. Sections include: what is a stroke? the stroke unit (Beech Ward, admission, visiting times, clothing, assessment of care, relative meetings, recreation); members of the ward team – who are they and what do they do? (the physiotherapist, on admission, the family, the dietician, the occupational therapist, eating, dressing, washing/bathing, toileting, domestic activities, social/home, perceptual, activities/games/treatment, home visits, the speech therapist, the psychologist, the social worker); terminology (hemiplegia, dysphasis, dysarthria, dyspraxia, dysphagia, dementia, hemianopia, perceptual problems); approaching discharge (programme leading up to discharge, placement, accommodation, rest homes, private nursing homes, cost, social service homes, long term care in hospital); services available after discharge (the day hospital, district nurses, the GP, stroke club, literature).

Patients' views

This leaflet was generally well received. Participants thought it contained useful and relevant information, especially for the families of people who have had a stroke. The explanations of what to expect in hospital and where to get help after rehabilitation in hospital were particularly appreciated. Omissions were sources of financial advice and support.

The leaflet was thought to be well written and clearly laid out, although some people thought it was too long. It was praised for giving the impression that the patient was an individual person.

Academic specialists' views

The specialist reviewers were much less enthusiastic than the patients about this leaflet. In the view of one it contained 'many omissions, typographical mistakes and some errors'. This leaflet, which includes some of the same material as the Stroke Association leaflet, is intended for patients admitted to a specific stroke unit. It describes what will happen once a patient is admitted to a specific stroke unit. Specialists noted that it made no attempt to present alternatives, but felt this may be due to the lack of availability of alternative services locally. For example, physiotherapy at home has been found to be cheaper and more effective than day hospital care, but it was not mentioned, possibly because it is not locally available.

The language and style of the leaflet was criticised: 'Difficult in parts. Switches from talking about the patient to talking to the patient. Dogmatic presentation of information, little indication given on any flexibility in the system'. 'Rather distant and full of jargon. Very *Guardian* and not much of *The Sun*, e.g. "If perceptual problems are not highlighted they may impede recovery". Inaccuracies were pointed out, including the following: 'Dysphasis should be dysphasia. Emotional lability is separate from dysarthria. Dementia and perceptual problems poorly described'; 'Dementia is *not* "a speech and language breakdown that usually occurs in the elderly". Hemianopia clumsily explained. "Rest homes" are called "residential homes".'

The booklet was criticised for failing to discuss the known benefits of rehabilitation, or of depression which is common in patients who have had strokes. Reviewers felt it did not provide the patient or their carer with sufficient information to facilitate informed choices. For example, information could have been provided on the pros and cons of early versus late use of a wheelchair, but this was not mentioned.

Stroke: South Manchester NHS Trust

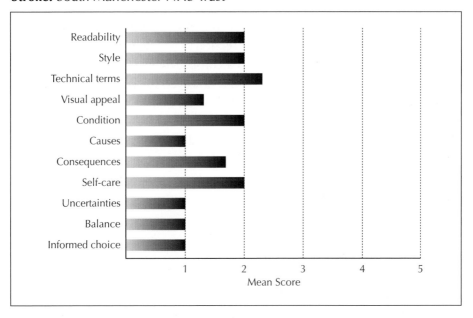

Why me? The experience of stroke (video): The Stroke Association

Overall ratings: Patients   7.7 (range 3–10) rank 4
                    Specialists   5.7 (range 3–9) rank 3

Publication date: 1984

Address: The Stroke Association, CHSA House, Whitecross
                    Street, London EC1Y 8JJ.

Description

A 24-minute video featuring three people who tell, in their own words, how
stroke has affected their lives. It is presented by Cliff Morgan, ex-rugby football
player, who himself suffered a stroke. Case studies include a retired upholsterer,
a housewife who had a stroke when she was 38, and a businessman.

Patients' views

Participants generally found this video relevant and liked the fact that it contained the real life stories of a cross section of people who had had a stroke. The fact that it addressed the emotional consequences of having a stroke was particularly appreciated. It was criticised, however, for not mentioning some treatments, such as electrical stimulation, and for being short on detail.

Participants were divided in their views about the presentation of the material. While some found the video optimistic and liked it, others thought it appeared rather outdated and depressing.

Academic specialists' views

Specialist reviewers were very divided in their opinions of this video. One liked it: 'This is an excellent video illustrating three experiences of stroke. Nice anecdotal data. The three patients described illustrate a good range of symptoms'. Another considered it more suitable for health professionals than for patients: 'Powerful, but not for patients'. The third found it negative: 'As a health care professional, I feel this video gives a very negative view of rehabilitation – certainly not evidence-based'.

The aim of the video is to describe patients' experiences rather than to provide comprehensive information on treatment options, so it does not cover treatment to reduce risk of further stroke, location of rehabilitation (hospital/home/stroke unit), or post-discharge care (rehabilitation, financial advice, etc.). One reviewer felt the patients were presented as passive recipients of care rather than as active participants. 'I do not know what the point of this video is. It presents a depressing picture if for patients. Is it for care staff or as an advert to highlight the need for the important work of the Stroke Association?' Another felt it was 'excellent in illustrating experience of stroke'.

Why me? The experience of stroke *(video):* Stroke Association

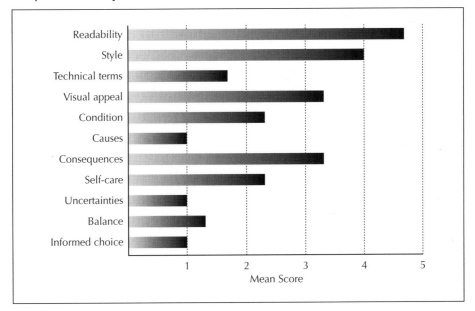

References

Ader D N, Seibring A R, Bhaskar P, Melamed B G (1992). Information seeking and interactive videodisc preparation for third molar extraction. *Journal of Oral Maxillofacial Surgery* 50: 27–31

Agbamu D A, Sim E (1997). Public health information on world wide web is hard to find. *British Medical Journal* 315: 1469

Arthur V A M (1995). Written patient information: a review of the literature. *Journal of Advanced Nursing* 21: 1081–6

Audit Commission (1993). *What seems to be the matter: communication between hospitals and patients*. London: HMSO

Balas E A, Austin S M, Mitchell J A, Ewigman B G, Bopp K D, Brown G D (1996). The clinical value of computerized information services: a review of 98 randomized controlled trials. *Archives of Family Medicine* 5: 271–278

Barry M J, Cherkin D C, Chang Y C, Fowler F J, Skates S (1997). A randomized trial of a multimedia shared decision-making program for men facing a treatment decision for benign prostatic hyperplasia. *Disease Management and Clinical Outcomes* 1: 5–14

Barry M J, Fowler F J, Mulley A G, Henderson J V, Wennberg J E (1995). Patient reactions to a program designed to facilitate patient participation in treatment decisions for benign prostatic hyperplasia. *Medical Care* 33: 771–82

Beaver K, Luker K A, Owens R G, Leinster S J, Degner L F (1996). Treatment decision-making in women newly diagnosed with breast cancer. *Cancer Nursing* 19: 8–19

Bernier M J (1996). Establishing the psychometric properties of a scale for evaluating quality in printed education materials. *Patient Education and Counseling* 29: 283–299

Bishop P, Kirwan J, Windsor K (1996). *The ARC patient literature evaluation project*. Arthritis and Rheumatism Council for Research in Great Britain and the Commonwealth

Blanchard C G, Labrecque M S, Ruckdeschel J C, Blanchard E B (1988). Information and decision-making preferences of hospitalized adult cancer patients. *Social Science and Medicine* 27: 1139–1145

Brody D S, Miller S M, Lerman C E, Smith D G, Caputo G (1989). Patient perception of involvement in medical care. *Journal of General Internal Medicine* 4: 506–511

Brown A, Armstrong D (1995). Telephone consultations in general practice: an additional or alternative service? *British Journal of General Practice* 45: 673–675

Brown S A (1988). Effects of educational interventions in diabetes care: a meta-analysis of findings. *Nursing Research* 37: 223–230

Brown S A (1990). Studies of educational interventions and outcomes in diabetic adults: a meta-analysis revisited. *Patient Education and Counseling* 16: 189–215

Bruster S, Jarman B, Bosanquet N, Weston D, Erens R, Delbanco T (1994). National survey of hospital patients. *British Medical Journal* 309: 1542–9

Buckland S, Gann B (1997). *Disseminating treatment outcomes information to consumers.* London: King's Fund

Calnan M, Katsouyiannopoulos V, Ovcharov V, Ramic H, Williams S (1994). Major determinants of consumer satisfaction with primary care in different health systems. *Family Practice* 11: 468-78

Carter W B, Beach L R, Inui T S (1986) The flu shot study: using multiattribute utility theory to design a vaccination intervention. *Organizational Behavior and Human Decision Processes* 38: 378–91

Cassileth B R, Zupkis R V, Sutton-Smith K, March V (1980). Information and participation preferences among cancer patients. *Annals of Internal Medicine* 92: 832–6

Chalmers I, Sackett D, Silagy C (1997). The Cochrane Collaboration. In: Maynard A, Chalmers I (eds). *Non-random reflections on health services research.* London: BMJ Publishing Group

Charles C, Gafni A, Whelan T (1997). Shared decision-making in the medical encounter: What does it mean? (or it takes at least two to tango). *Social Science and Medicine* 44: 681–692

Cockburn J, Pit S (1997). Prescribing behaviour in clinical practice: patients' expectations and doctors' perceptions of patients' expectations – a questionnaire study. *British Medical Journal* 315: 520–3

Contento I, Balch G I, Bronner Y L, Lytle L A, Maloney S K, Olsen C M, Swadener S S (1995). The effectiveness of nutrition education and implications for nutrition education policy, programs and research: a review of research. *Journal of Nutrition Education* 27: 277–418

Coulter A (1997). Partnerships with patients: the pros and cons of shared clinical decision-making. *Journal of Health Services Research and Policy* 2: 112–21

Coulter A, Peto V, Doll H (1994). Patients' preferences and general practitioners' decisions in the treatment of menstrual disorders. *Family Practice* 11: 67–74

Deber R B (1994). The patient-physician partnership: changing roles and the desire for information. *Canadian Medical Association Journal* 151: 171–6

Deber R B, Kraetschmer N, Irvine J (1996). What role do patients wish to play in treatment decision-making? *Archives of Internal Medicine* 156:1414–20

Department of Health (1992). The *Patient's Charter*. London: HMSO

Devine E C (1992). Effects of psychoeducational care for adult surgical patients: a meta-analysis of 191 studies. *Patient Education and Counseling* 19: 129–42

Division of Public Health and Primary Care, University of Oxford (1998). *The DISCERN handbook: quality criteria for consumer health information*. Oxford: Radcliffe Medical Press

Eiser J R, Eiser C (1996). *Effectiveness of video for health education: a review*. London: Health Education Authority

Emanuel E J, Emanuel I L (1992). Four models of the physician-patient relationship. *Journal of the American Medical Association* 267: 2221–6

England S L, Evans J (1992). Patients' choices and perceptions after an invitation to participate in treatment decisions. *Social Science and Medicine* 34: 1217–25

Entwistle V, Watt I S, Herring J E (1996a). *Information about health care effectiveness*. London: King's Fund

Entwistle V A, Sheldon T A, Sowden A J, Watt I S (1996b). Supporting consumer involvement in decision-making: what constitutes quality in consumer health information? *International Journal for Quality in Health Care* 8: 425–37

Entwistle V A, Watt I S, Davis H, Dickson R, Pickard D, Rosser J (1998). Developing information materials to present the findings of technology assessments to consumers. International Journal of Technology Assessment in Health Care 14: 47–70

Entwistle V A, Watt I S, Sowden A J (1997). Information to facilitate patient involvement in decision-making – some issues. *Journal of Clinical Effectiveness* 2: 69–72

Fallowfield L J, Hall A, Maguire G P, Baum M (1990). Psychological outcomes of different treatment policies in women with early breast cancer outside a clinical trial. *British Medical Journal* 301: 575–80

Flood A B, Wennberg J E, Nease R F, Fowler F J, Ding J, Hynes L M (1996). The importance of patient preference in the decision to screen for prostate cancer. *Journal of General Internal Medicine* 11: 342–9

Gibbs S, Waters W E, George C F (1989). The benefits of prescription information leaflets. *British Journal of Clinical Pharmacology* 27: 723–39

Gibson P G, Coughlan J, Wilson A J, Hensley M J, Abramson M, Bauman A, Walters E H (1998). The effects of limited (information only) patient education programs on the health outcomes of adults with asthma. *The Cochrane Library*, Issue 1.

Hallam L (1993). Access to general practice and general practitioners by telephone: the patient's view. *British Journal of General Practice* 43: 331–5

Hannay D R (1979). *The symptom iceberg – a study of community health.* London: Routledge and Kegan Paul.

Hawkey G M, Hawkey C J (1989). Effect of information leaflets on knowledge in patients with gastrointestinal diseases. *Gut* 30: 1641–6

Health Education Authority (1994). *Health-related resources for black and minority ethnic groups.* London: Health Education Authority

Health Education Authority (1995). *Health-related resources for people with learning disabilities.* London: Health Education Authority

Health Education Authority (1997). *Health-related resources for older people*. London: Health Education Authority

Healton C G, Messeri P (1993). The effect of video interventions on improving knowledge and treatment compliance in the sexually transmitted disease clinic setting. *Sexually Transmitted Diseases* 20: 70–6

Hopper K D, Zajdel M, Hulse S F, Yoanidis N R, TenHave T R, Labuski M R, Houts P S, Brensinger C M, Hartman D S (1994). Interactive method of informing patients of the risks of intravenous contrast media. *Radiology* 192: 67–71

Impicciatore P, Pandolfini C, Casella N, Bonati M (1997). Reliability of health information for the public on the world wide web: systematic survey of advice on managing fever in children at home. *British Medical Journal* 314: 1875–81

Jadad A R, Gagliardi A (1998). Rating health information on the Internet: navigating to knowledge or to Babel? *Journal of the American Medical Association* 279: 611–14

Kaplan S H, Greenfield S, Ware J E (1989). Assessing the effects of physician-patient interactions on the outcomes of chronic disease. *Medical Care* 27 (suppl): S110–S127

Kasper J F, Mulley A G, Wennberg J E (1992). Developing shared decision-making programs to improve the quality of health care. *Quality Review Bulletin* 18: 182–90

Kay E J, Locker D (1996). Is dental health education effective? A systematic review of current evidence. *Community Dentistry and Oral Epidemiology* 24: 231–5

Kemper D W (1997). *Healthwise Handbook* (13th ed.) Boise, Idaho: Healthwise Inc.

Kiely B G, McPherson I G (1986). Stress self-help packages in primary care: a controlled trial evaluation. *Journal of the Royal College of General Practitioners* 36: 307–9

Kieschnick T, Adler L J, Jimison H B (1996). *Health informatics directory*. Baltimore: Williams and Wilkins

Kok G, van den Borne B, Mullen P D (1997). Effectiveness of health education and health promotion: meta-analyses of effect studies and determinants of effectiveness. *Patient Education and Counseling* 30: 19–27

Laine C, Davidoff F (1996). Patient-centered medicine: a professional evolution. Journal of the American Medical Association 275: 152–6

Lerman C, Ross E, Boyce A, Gorchov P M, McLaughlin R, Rimer B, Engstrom P (1992). The impact of mailing psychoeducational materials to women with abnormal mammograms. *American Journal of Public Health* 82: 729–30

Lerman C E, Brody D S, Caputo G C, Smith D G, Lazaro C G, Wolfson H G (1990). Patients' perceived involvement in care scale: relationship to attitudes about illness and medical care. *Journal of General Internal Medicine* 5: 29–33

Levine M N, Gafni A, Markham B, MacFarlane D (1992). A bedside decision instrument to elicit a patient's preference concerning adjuvant chemotherapy for breast cancer. *Annals of Internal Medicine* 117: 53–8

Ley P (1988). *Communicating with patients: improving communication, satisfaction and compliance*. London: Croom Helm

Liao L, Jollis J G, DeLong E R, Peterson E D, Morris K G, Mark D B (1996). Impact of an interactive video on decision-making of patients with ischemic heart disease. *Journal of General Internal Medicine* 11: 373–6

Lorig K, Fries J (1995). The arthritis helpbook (4th ed). Addison-Wesley

Macfarlane J T, Holmes W F, Macfarlane R M (1997). Reducing reconsultations for acute lower respiratory tract illness with an information leaflet: a randomized controlled study of patients in primary care. *British Journal of General Practice* 47: 719–22

Malenka D J, Baron J D, Johansen S, Wahrenberger J W, Ross J M (1993). The framing effect of relative and absolute risk. *Journal of General Internal Medicine* 8: 543–8

Marklund B, Koritz P, Bjorkander E, Bengtsson C (1991). How well do nurse-run telephone consultations and consultations in the surgery agree? Experience in Swedish primary health care. *British Journal of General Practice* 41: 462–5

Mazur D J, Merz J F (1993). How the manner of presentation of data influences older patients in determining their treatment preferences. *Journal of the American Geriatric Society* 41: 223–8

Meade C D, Diekmann J, Thornhill D G (1992). Readability of American Cancer Society patient education literature. *Oncology Nursing Forum* 19: 51–5

Meade C D, Smith C F (1991). Readability formulas: cautions and criteria. *Patient Education and Counseling* 17: 153–8

Meredith P, Emberton M, Wood C, Smith J (1995). Comparison of patients' needs for information on prostate surgery with printed materials provided by surgeons. *Quality in Health Care* 4: 18–23

Mullen P D, Green L W, Persinger G S (1985). Clinical trials of patient education for chronic conditions: a comparative meta-analysis of intervention types. *Preventive Medicine* 14: 753–781

Mullen P D, Mains D A, Velez R (1992). A meta-analysis of controlled trials of cardiac patient education. *Patient Education and Counseling* 19: 143–62

Mumford M E (1997). A descriptive study of the readability of patient information leaflets designed by nurses. *Journal of Advanced Nursing* 26: 985–91

NHS Centre for Reviews & Dissemination (1995). *Review of the research on the effectiveness of health service interventions to reduce variations in health.* CRD Report 3. York: University of York

NHS Executive (1996). *Patient partnership: building a collaborative strategy.* London: Department of Health

National Health Service in Scotland (1991). *The Patient's Charter: a charter for health.* Edinburgh: Scottish Office

Nielsen E, Sheppard M A (1988). Television as a patient education tool: a review of its effectiveness. *Patient Education and Counseling* 11: 3–16

Niewijk A H, Weijts W B M (1997). Effects of a multi-media course on urinary incontinence. *Patient Education and Counseling* 30: 95–103

North East Thames Regional Health Authority (1994). *Making it happen: a guide to two-way patient information.* London: North East Thames Regional Health Authority

Osman L M, Abdalla M I, Beattie J A G, Ross S J, Russell I T, Friend J A, Legge J S, Douglas J G (1994). Reducing hospital admission through computer supported education for asthma patients. *British Medical Journal* 308: 568–71

Padgett D, Mumford E, Hynes M, Carter R (1988). Meta-analysis of the effects of educational and psychosocial interventions on management of diabetes mellitus. *Journal of Clinical Epidemiology* 41: 1007–30

Quill T E (1983). Partnerships in patient care: a contractual approach. *Annals of Internal Medicine* 98: 228–34

Rainey L C (1985). Effects of preparatory patient education for radiation oncology patients. *Cancer* 56: 1056–61

Richards M A, Ramirez A J, Degner L F, Fallowfield L J, Maher E J, Neuberger J (1995). Offering choice of treatment to patients with cancers. *European Journal of Cancer* 31A: 112–16

Rippen H E (1997). Criteria for assessing the quality of health information on the Internet. Mitretek Systems, http://www.mitretek.org

Ritchie J, Spencer L (1994). Qualitative data analysis for applied policy research. In: Bryman A, Burgess R (eds). *Analyzing qualitative data*. London: Routledge, pp 173–94

Roland M, Dixon M (1989). Randomised controlled trial of an educational booklet for patients presenting with back pain in general practice. *Journal of the Royal College of General Practitioners* 39: 244–6

Schulman B A (1979). Active patient orientation and outcomes in hypertensive treatment. *Medical Care* 17: 267–80

Secker J, Pollard R (1995). *Writing leaflets for patients: guidelines for written information*. Edinburgh: Health Education Board for Scotland

Secretary of State for Health (1997). *The new NHS*. London: The Stationery Office

Silberg W M, Lundberg G D, Musacchio R A (1997). Assessing, controlling, and assuring the quality of medical information on the internet. *Journal of the American Medical Association* 277: 1244–5

Simons-Morton D G, Mullen P D, Mains D A, Tabak E R, Green L W (1992). Characteristics of controlled studies of patient education and counseling for preventive health behaviors. *Patient Education and Counseling* 19: 175–204

Simpson M, Buckman R, Stewart M, Maguire P, Lipkin M, Novack D, Till J (1991). *Doctor-patient communication: the Toronto consensus statement*. British Medical Journal 303: 1385–7

Sitzia J, Wood N (1997). Patient satisfaction: a review of issues and concepts. *Social Science and Medicine* 45: 1829–43

Stewart D E, Buchegger P M, Lickrish G M, Sierra S (1994). The effect of educational brochures on follow-up compliance in women with abnormal papanicolaou smears. *Obstetrics and Gynecology* 83: 583–5

Stewart M A (1995). Effective physician-patient communication and health outcomes: a review. Canadian Medical Association Journal 152: 1423–33

Strull W M, Lo B, Charles G (1984). Do patients want to participate in medical decision-making? *Journal of the American Medical Association* 252: 2990–4

Sutherland H J, Llewellyn-Thomas H A, Lockwood G A, Tritchler D L, Till J E (1989). Cancer patients: their desire for information and participation in treatment decisions. *Journal of the Royal Society of Medicine* 82: 260–3

Szasz T S, Hollender M H (1956). A contribution to the philosophy of medicine. *Archives of Internal Medicine* 97: 585–92

Update Software (1998). *The Cochrane Library*. Oxford: Cochrane Centre

Vahabi M, Ferris L (1995). Improving written patient education materials: a review of the evidence. *Health Education Journal* 54: 99–106

Veatch R M (1972) Models for ethical medicine in a revolutionary age: What physician-patient roles foster the most ethical relationship? *Hastings Center Report* 2: 5–7

Vickery D M, Kalmer H, Lowry D, Constantine M, Wright E, Loren W (1983). Effect of a self-care education program on medical visits. *Journal of the Americal Medical Association* 250: 2952–6

Wagner E H, Barrett P, Barry M J, Barlow W, Fowler F J (1995). The effect of a shared decision-making program on rates of surgery for benign prostatic hyperplasia. *Medical Care* 33: 765–70

Wallace S (1996). The future's bright: the future's digital. London: King's Fund

Watkins C J, Papacosta A O, Chinn S, Martin J (1987). A randomized controlled trial of an information booklet for hypertensive patients in general practice. *Journal of the Royal College of General Practitioners* 37: 548–50

Whelan T J, Levine M N, Gafni A, Lukka H, Mohide E A, Patel M, Streiner D L (1995). Breast irradiation postlumpectomy: development and evaluation of a decision instrument. *Journal of Clinical Oncology* 13: 847–53

Williams S, Crouch R, Dale J (1995). Providing health care advice by telephone. *Professional Nurse* 10: 750–2

Wolf A M, Nasser J F, Wolf A M, Schorling J B (1996). Impact of informed consent on patient interest in prostate-specific antigen. *Archives of Internal Medicine* 156: 1333–6

Wyatt J C (1997). Measuring quality and impact of the world wide web. *British Medical Journal* 314: 1879–81

Yanovski S, Yanovski J, Malley J, Brown R, Balaban D (1992). Telephone triage by primary care physicians. *Pediatrics* 89: 701–6

Appendix

Focus group topic guide

Key research objectives

- Ascertain what factors determine good quality information material for people facing treatment decisions
- How information material can help decision-making
- Evaluate specific information materials currently available about treatment options and outcomes

Introduction

- *SCPR independent research institute* ... commissioned to conduct research on many social issues – health/unemployment/education etc.
- On this occasion asked to assist in a project for the King's Fund – an independent charity promoting research and information on good practice in health care
- *Project aim* is to identify factors which determine good quality information material for patients who are thinking about treatment options. Talking to both health professionals and patients for the research study. Conducting ten group discussions amongst different patient groups
- *Purpose of discussion* to consult patients on what they need from patient information materials when they are deciding between treatment options and to get patients' views on some specific examples
- *About the discussion*: unable to answer medical questions: tape recording – to save writing down – but anonymous: how the discussion works – go round the table once to introduce everyone – then discussion

1. Background information (round the table)

Age, household composition, working status, membership of health organisation, where they are from   (10 min)

2. Condition (briefly)

Introduction: As you know, everybody in this group is here because they have had or are being currently treated for ... The main purpose of the discussion, as we've said, is to talk about information material. But before we go on to discuss that it would be helpful, without going into detail, to talk a little more about your condition.

- How long have they had ...?
- What treatments have they tried?
- Who recommended/decided which treatments should be tried? **(10 min)**

3. Use of information materials in making decisions about treatments

- Were they given treatment options?
- How involved did they feel in the choice of treatment?
- How were they informed of treatment options?
- How aware were they of information materials available?
- Which information sources have they used to find out about treatments?
  – professionals
  – written information: leaflets/reference books/medical textbooks
  – video
  – cassettes
  – support groups, etc.
- Which information source do they prefer? why?
- What other information did they need?
- How well informed do they feel they are?
- Any unmet needs? what have been the consequences? **(15 min)**

4. The role of information materials

- When they first became aware of their condition what did they need to know?
- How do needs change over the course of their condition
- What role do information materials play in informing the patient, for example:
  – providing general information about the condition (causes and consequences)
  – as a reminder of professional advice
  – to help patients make choices (risks and benefits) **(10 min)**

5. Reactions to information materials sent

Taking each information material in turn:
- what rating did they give it overall? why?
- what were their initial reactions to it?
- what were its strengths/weaknesses?
- did it hold their attention? why? why not?
- what did they see as its key message?
- what types of people did they feel it was aimed at?
- at what stage would it have helped?
- what are their views on the information materials in terms of:

Language, i.e.
accessibility
comprehensibility
style/tone ..... is it jargonistic? technical? medical? patronising?
how readable is it?

Presentation, i.e.
impact (e.g. front cover – did it hold their attention? how much did they take in?)
structure
layout/signposting
quality of paper
colour
typeface
use of illustrations/photographs

Usefulness/Content, i.e.
did it tell them anything new?
how relevant is it to them?
does it cover all the treatment options?
is the level of detail appropriate?
does it say enough about causes and consequences?
does it say enough about risks and benefits?

Helping decision-making, i.e.
providing options/choices
encouraging involvement in decision-making (implicit/explicit)

Credibility, i.e.
    trustworthiness
    where they aware who produced it? what effect did this have?

    – what rating do they give it now?
    – discuss reasons for change
    – what improvements would they like to see?
    – where should it be available?

After discussing each of the information materials:
- which did they prefer overall? why?
- which did they least prefer? why?
- overall, what factors make a good information leaflet?

                                   (7 min on each)

6. Comparison of media

- What role do audio-cassettes/videos serve versus information leaflets?
- What are the advantages of audio-cassettes/video?
- What are the disadvantages of audio-cassettes/video?
- In what circumstances would audio-cassettes/video be used?
- Which do they prefer as an information source? why?
- Where should different types of information materials be available?
- Which of the information materials would they recommend to others facing treatment options?   **(10 min)**

Academic specialists' checklist

Section A: Overall rating

1. Overall, what rating would you give this booklet? (*hint: please give a mark out of ten based on your **initial impressions** of the booklet*)

MARK: /10

please give reasons for your rating:

Please note that there are further questions below concerning your assessment of this booklet.

Section B: About the clinical condition

2. How good is the booklet at giving patients **general information about the condition**? (*hint: does it give basic information about the nature of the condition, symptoms? prevalence? etc.*)

Poor   1   2   3   4   5   Excellent

please give reasons for your rating:

3. How good is the booklet at giving patients information about the **causes** of the condition (e.g. biomedical, psycho-social, environmental, genetic)

    Poor   1   2   3   4   5   **Excellent**

please give reasons for your rating:

4. How good is the booklet at giving patients information about the **consequences** of the condition?

    Poor   1   2   3   4   5   **Excellent**

please give reasons for your rating:

Section C: About treatment options and diagnostic interventions

5. In the following table please list the **treatment options and diagnostic interventions** included in this booklet. For each please assess **how well the content matches the known facts.** The scale utilised should be as follows:

    Poor   1   2   3   4   5   **Excellent**

Please include **diagnostic, medical, surgical and non-medical alternatives** (such as watchful waiting, self-help, lifestyle changes, talking treatments, complementary therapies)

Type of treatment	Information about benefits (a) what they are	Information about benefits (b) chances of them happening	Information about risks (a) what they are	Information about risks (b) chances of them happening	Comments
example: Surgery	3	3	(excellent) 5	(poor) 1	gives idea of main benefits, but not others (e.g. ...); lists common and rare complications, but no detail of frequency (e.g. ....)

6. Does the material omit any **treatment options**

      YES / NO

if yes, what are they?

7. How good is the booklet at giving patients information about **lifestyle changes, coping strategies or self-care?**

    Poor   1   2   3   4   5   **Excellent**

please give reasons for your rating:

8. How good is the booklet at portraying **uncertainties or gaps in knowledge?**

    Poor   1   2   3   4   5   **Excellent**

please give reasons for your rating:

9. How good is the booklet at presenting a **balanced view** of the different treatment options? (*hint: is there a bias in the coverage of information about different treatment options, for example, in the way in which options are described, the order of presentation, highlighted emphasis?*)

    Poor   1   2   3   4   5   **Excellent**

please give reasons for your rating:

Section D: Presentation

10. Please give your overall impressions about the **comprehensibility** and **readability** of the language.

Poor	1	2	3	4	5	**Excellent**

please give reasons for your rating:

11. What are your overall impressions of the **style and tone** with which the booklet is written? (*hint: is the tone direct? friendly? patronising? concise? conversational? use active or passive verbs?*)

Poor	1	2	3	4	5	**Excellent**

please give reasons for your rating:

12. How good is the booklet at **explaining technical terms**? (*hint: does it explain technical terms clearly? accurately?*)

Poor	1	2	3	4	5	**Excellent**

please give reasons for your rating:

13. Please give your overall impressions about the **visual appeal** of the material (*hint: what are your thoughts on layout, attractiveness, use of illustrations, graphics, highlighting, emphasis on most important information, etc.?*)

Poor   1   2   3   4   5   **Excellent**

please give reasons for your rating:

Section E: Overall comments

14. How good is the booklet at giving patients the information they need in order to make **informed choices** about treatment options?

Poor   1   2   3   4   5   **Excellent**

What factors most influenced your rating?

15. How could it be **improved**?

16. Do you have any **further comments** about the material?

17. Please could you let us know if you have been involved in the production of this booklet. Or any others? If so, in what capacity?

18. Having completed the checklist, what overall rating would you now give this booklet?

MARK: /10

please give reasons for any changes in your rating:

Please return completed checklist by Friday, 21 February 1997

Publishers' questionnaire

Title:

Format:

Produced by:

Publication date:

A. Background facts

1. Please could you give us details of the people primarily responsible for producing and authoring the material.

2. Is the leaflet due to be revised? If so, when?

B. Aims and objectives

3. Please could you explain the **main aims and objectives** of the leaflet (e.g. is it meant to provide background information about the clinical condition, to explain the different treatments, etc.)

4. **For what sort of patients or users** is it designed to be used? (i.e. is it aimed at particular sub-groups of users in this clinical field, for a particular gender, age-group etc.?)

5. How is the leaflet meant to be **disseminated or used in practice**? (e.g. in primary care, secondary care, to be given out by GPs during a consultation, by a specialist after referral etc.?)

C. Production and evaluation

6. Please could you describe the **process by which the leaflet was produced** (e.g. how was the content of the leaflet decided upon? what sources of information were utilised? how was the format and presentation decided upon, etc.)

7. Please could you describe **how patients or users have been involved** in the production of the leaflet (e.g. by taking part in focus groups to identify what should be included in the leaflet, as authors commenting on draft versions, etc.)

8. Please could you describe **how clinical experts or subject specialists have been involved** (e.g. by evaluating drafts? as authors? etc.)

9. Has the leaflet been **evaluated** following its production (e.g. through surveys on what people think about it, or via formal assessments of its impact in practice, etc.)

10. Are there any other comments you would like to make about the production of this leaflet?

**Please return in the envelope provided to
David Gilbert, Research Officer, MICE,
King's Fund, 11–13 Cavendish Square, London WIM 0AN
or fax: 0171 307 2810**

Focus group participants

Mrs J. Adie
Mrs J. Balogun
Mr A. Barwell
Ms S. Boazman
Mrs S. Britten
Mrs L. Brown
Ms L. Bryant
Mrs D. Cavett
Ms A. Cherrie
Miss H. Clarke
Mr H. Clarke
Mr R. Cooper
Mr K. Cowley
Ms B. Crockett
Mrs C. Dickins
Mr S. Dodge
Mrs L. Drinkwater
Mrs S. Edwards
Ms M. Ellis
Mr P. Embleton
Mrs A. Erskine
Ms J. Faulkner
Mrs C. Gardner
Miss M. Grice
Mrs C. Hackett
Mr P. Harding
Mrs M. J. Harris
Mrs B. Hindley
Mr D. Hobson
Mr J. Horsfall
Ms P. Hughes
Mrs J. Huggard

Mr J. James
Mr J. Jeffery
Mr R. Jenks
Mr K. Khan
Mrs J. Lawes
Mrs J. Marshall
Mrs C. Marvel
Mrs S. Monger
Mrs G. Morar
Mrs M. Nicholson
Ms R. Nightingale
Mrs V. Peacock
Mrs C. Pedder
Mr T. Pilkington
Mr D. Postlethwaite
Ms J. Premdas
Mrs J. Pye
Mr A. Richer
Mr C. Roberts
Ms M. Roberts
Mrs P. Roy
Mrs J. Short
Mr G. Sivewright
Mr E. Stillwell
Mrs G. Sturgeon-Lewis
Mrs J. Thorne
Mrs M. Underwood
Ms L. Wayne
Mrs M. Wilson
Ms B. Wilmer
Mr C. Wylie

Clinical and academic specialists

Dr David Baldwin, Department of Psychiatry, University of Southampton

Prof. Nick Black, Department of Public Health and Policy, London School of Hygiene and Tropical Medicine

Prof. John Bonnar, Woodstock, Oxford

Dr Katherine Brogan, NHS Executive Anglia and Oxford

Mr Christopher Bulstrode, Nuffield Orthopaedic Centre, University of Oxford

Prof. George Davey-Smith, Department of Social Medicine, University of Bristol

Mr Mark Emberton, Institute of Urology, Middlesex Hospital, London

Dr Gene Feder, Department of General Practice and Primary Care, St Bartholomew's and the Royal London School of Medicine and Dentistry, London

Prof. Ray Fitzpatrick, Department of Public Health and Primary Care, University of Oxford

Dr Anne Forster, School of Health Care Studies, University of Leeds and Department of Health Care for the Elderly, Bradford

Prof. Mark Haggard, MRC Institute of Hearing Research, Nottingham University

Dr Sally Hope, Woodstock, Oxford

Prof. Michael King, Department of Psychiatry, Royal Free Hospital School of Medicine, London

Dr Malcolm Law, Wolfson Institute of Preventive Medicine, St Bartholomew's and the Royal London School of Medicine and Dentistry, London

Dr David Lawrence, Public Health Department, Ealing, Hammersmith and Hounslow Health Authority

Dr Richard Lindley, Department of Clinical Neurosciences, University of Edinburgh

Prof. Klim McPherson, Department of Public Health and Policy, London School of Hygiene and Tropical Medicine

Mr Richard Maw, St Michael's Hospital, Bristol

Dr Jennifer Moffett, University of Hull Institute of Rehabilitation, Hull

Prof. David E Neal, Department of Surgery, University of Newcastle

Mr Hugh Phillips, Norwich, Norfolk

Prof. L E Ramsay, Department of Clinical Pharmacology and Therapeutics, Royal Hallamshire Hospital, Sheffield

Dr Margaret Rees, Department of Obstetrics and Gynaecology, John Radcliffe Hospital, University of Oxford

Prof. Martin Roland, National Primary Care Research and Development Centre, University of Manchester

Prof. Templeton, Department of Obstetrics and Gynaecology, Aberdeen University

Dr Derick T. Wade, Rivermead Rehabilitation Centre, Oxford

Dr Simon Wessely, Reader in Psychological Medicine, King's College School of Medicine, University of London

Dr Richard Wormald, Glaxo Department of Ophthalmic Epidemiology, Moorfields Eye Hospital